D1591504

MOSER—ARTISTRY IN GLASS
1857-1938

by
Gary Baldwin &
Lee Carno

This book is dedicated to those designers and artisans who, through an untiring dedication to excellence, have bequeathed to the world the legacy of Moser glass.

ACKNOWLEDGEMENTS

In grateful recognition of their valuable assistance in making this book possible, the authors wish to thank Mrs. Ursula Schubert for her translation and interpretation of what appeared to be an endless series of German articles; personnel at the Corning Museum of Glass, and, in particular, Mrs. Norma Jenkins who was most helpful in the gathering of pertinent information; Mr. Peter Rath of J&L Lobmeyr and Dr. Alena Adlerová of the Prague Museum of Decorative Arts for their aid in resolving several controversial issues; the Moser family for providing historical background information heretofore unavailable in the open literature; and Mr. and Mrs. Richard Flagg, whose editing and helpful discussions were invaluable in the organization of the manuscript. We also wish to express our gratitude to the numerous collectors of Moser glass, both recognized and anonymous, who provided the extensive sampling of glass types recorded here and whose stimulating discussions and observations contributed greatly to our understanding of the subject matter contained within these pages. Finally, but certainly not least, we wish to acknowledge the significant contributions of our respective spouses without whose understanding, assistance and patience this text would remain but a noble dream.

Table of Contents

FOREWORD

Moser is a name recognized and respected by contemporary glass collectors as representing a combination of technical excellence and unique decorative design. Over the years, the Moser name has become associated with a select category of decorative styles. However, relatively little is known about Ludwig Moser, the glass industry founded and developed by him, or the extensive variety of glassware actually produced by the Moser factory.

Moser—Artistry in Glass (1857-1938) presents historical background and design information obtained from currently available sources. This knowledge has been organized to enhance understanding of the multiple factors which influenced Moser production. For the sake of clarity, we have classified Moser decorative styles according to their recognizable characteristics. Carefully selected photographs have been included to illustrate the beauty and rich variety of artistic glass marketed by the Moser firm.

INTRODUCTION

Published works describing Central European glass production during the latter half of the 19th and first part of the 20th centuries are largely absent from American libraries. Although a considerable number of books and periodicals have been written on this subject, a perceived lack of interest on the part of American collectors has prevented widespread translation of many German texts.

From approximately 1870 to 1938, Central European glasshouses marketed a prodigious variety of luxury glass. Unfortunately, only a small sampling of that output was recorded by contemporary glass historians, and many factory records were subsequently destroyed by the ravages of war. In contrast to the American glass industry which, from a historical and design standpoint, has been reasonably well documented, the intricacies of the Central European glass industry during this period offer an unparalleled opportunity to those interested in the field of investigative journalism. In writing this book, the authors have organized historical and design information about the Moser firm in such a way as to stimulate, it is hoped, an American renaissance of interest in the fascinating history of Central European glass production. We cannot overstate the importance of this knowledge to those interested in American glass, for it is here that many underlying factors which directly influenced American decorative styles are to be found.

In much the same way that an artist paints on canvas, the term "artistic glass" implies the use of surface decorative techniques such as engraving, cutting or enameling. Pure art glass, on the other hand, relies on the color, texture and form of the glass medium for its visual appeal. The ability to meld these two artistic concepts into a mutually complementary art·form represents one of the highest achievements in the field of decorative glass. The firm founded by Ludwig Moser achieved such artistry.

Prior to 1895, Moser artists were acknowledged masters at adapting the themes of romantic painters, as well as Bohemian Renaissance, Baroque and naturalistic motifs, to create distinctively decorated enameled artware. With the completion of his own glassmaking facilities in 1895, Ludwig Moser's lifelong dream of creating a perfect glass medium to complement his decorative styles was finally realized. Deeply engraved Art Nouveau glass, popular during the 1895-1905 period, was produced by Moser with techniques adopted from Bohemian seal and gem cutters. Created from highly refined shaded blanks colored by newly developed Moser glasses, this glass rapidly achieved international recognition. Moser's adaptation of Jan Kotêra's modern concepts in glass cutting and design resulted in an extensive selection of distinctive glassware styles which are as popular today as when they were first introduced.

After World War I, the Moser firm significantly expanded its marketing of enamaled glassware. Although based on traditional decorative themes, this new line of artistic glass exhibited a definite stylistic change from earlier work. Partly as the result of Moser's purchase of Meyr's Neffe's Adolf works in 1922, the enameled glass produced by Moser in the ensuing two decades reached a degree of balance and technical execution unsurpassed in the firm's existence. Perhaps Moser's most important contribution to the world of artistic glass occurred in 1922 when Leo Moser introduced a series of colored rare-earth doped glasses. Combined with facet-cutting techniques designed to emphasize the jewel-like properties of the multicolored glass medium, these new glasses resulted in the Moser firm's being awarded top honors at international exhibitions.

During a relatively short period of 38 years, beginning with the completion of Moser's Meierhöfen works in 1895 and terminating with the total acquisition of the firm by the Bohemian Union Bank in 1933, Moser glass rose to the international pinnacle of success. As the result of the firm's dedication to artistic and technical standards of the highest possible level, the quality of the crystal mass and the perfection of cut were unsurpassed by any other contemporary glasshouse. Moser glass became the cherished possession of royalty and other important personages throughout the world and was justifiably referred to as the "Glass of Kings."

In writing this book the authors have attempted to provide the reader with as comprehensive a historical record as can be obtained from available sources. Considerable historical information has been obtained from articles published in the *Czech Glass Review,* as well as from German books and records contemporary with the time period of interest. Much of the narrative regarding Ludwig Moser's early years was derived from records brought to this country by Leo Moser and retained by the Corning Museum of Glass. Biographical sketches on Leo and Richard Moser appear in print for the first time and are largely a result of personal interviews with members of the Moser family.

Moser glass has long been an enigma to many glass collectors. Certainly the Moser name has been recognized as connoting high quality, but for all but a select few an understanding of the broad scope of Moser products has remained illusive. As an aid to the process of identification we have segregated the majority of Moser glass into generic categories based on prominent decorative features and/or techniques. This approach is based on a foundation of glass items known to be of Moser origin and should prove quite valuable in the identification of pieces heretofore lacking proper attribution. Further aids in attribution are provided by a summary of the technical characteristics exhibited by Moser glass, including information regarding glass types and construction techniques.

We have identified geographical locations throughout Bohemia, using the names appropriate to the time frame in which they are mentioned. Prior to 1918, many of the prominent glassmaking centers bore German names; after the fall of the Austro-Hungarian Empire, these names were replaced by Czech equivalents. When both German and Czech forms are known to the authors, they are included for clarity.

I. KARLSBAD—ELEVATION TO INTERNATIONAL PROMINENCE

Bohemia had established itself as a leader in Central European glass production as early as the second half of the 14th century. There is evidence that even in this early period limited amounts of Bohemian glassware were being exported to foreign markets. From these humble beginnings emerged what was perhaps the most extensive network of glass exporting facilities yet recorded. By the latter half of the 17th century, Ceská Lípa was recognized as the foremost Bohemian center of glass manufacturing and trade. Engravers and enamelists, operating either as private individuals or out of small shops, decorated glass bought from the major factories. The finished products were then exported or sold at the major centers of commerce located throughout Bohemia.

Continuing success in the export of Bohemian glass was ensured after 1750 by the construction of permanent warehouses in all of the important ports and cities in Europe, as well as overseas. To cultivate foreign markets, advanced sales and display techniques were used to attract wealthy and influential buyers. Special sales rooms were established in important towns, and trade people and the nobility were invited to inspect the displayed glassware. At these locations, demonstrations of engraving and enameling techniques were frequently arranged. Individual artists traveled about the countryside carrying with them the equipment necessary to produce customized decorations such as inscriptions, monograms or coats of arms. In addition, shops were set up in the heavily frequented spa areas to service wealthy patrons.

Bohemian glass production experienced a rapid growth during the 18th century. In 1753, 58 glassworks are known to have been in operation; by 1799, this total increased to 79 with approximately 3,000 people being employed. Records show that 8,209 metric tons of glass were exported to foreign markets in 1805; the number reached 23,780 metric tons in 1825. During this period the traditional customers of Bohemia were Turkey, Spain, Portugal, the German states and Northern Italy. In 1855, 83 glass houses were active in Bohemia. These houses produced three-fifths of all the glass manufactured in the Austrian state, and employed some 120,000 workers. Principal manufacturers were Harrach in Neuwelt (Nový Svêt) and Meyr's Neffe* in Winterberg (Vimperk) and Eleonorenhain. Luxury glass produced by these firms was primarily exported to England, Germany, Switzerland and Italy.

Karlsbad (Karlovy Vary), a renowned spa dating from the 17th century and presently capital of Czechoslovakia's Karlovy Vary province, is situated 1,225 feet above sea level at the intersection of the Tepel and Eger rivers. As illustrated in an early view by the artist L. Buquoy, Karlsbad appears to cling to the foothills of the precipitous Erzgebirge Range as it rises tier upon tier above the valley floor. Known chiefly for the curative properties of no less than 17 warm springs, Karlsbad attracted nobility and wealthy patrons from all over the world. These springs, ranging in temperature from 108 to 164°F, and believed to originate from a common reservoir, are free from any color or odor and are consequently used for both drinking and bathing. The chemical composition of the spring water is considered valuable in the treatment of liver diseases and ailments produced by uric acid. These waters were thought so potent that special medical and treatment centers were established to properly administer their medicinal properties.

Spa waters were first used for bathing in 1520, but the rapid growth of the town as an international health resort dates from the middle of the 19th century. Much of this success was the responsibility of the renowned physician Jean de Carro (1770-1857), whose tireless efforts as a champion of the adoption of vaccination brought him world-wide acclaim. From

*Spelling appears as Meyr's Neffe on the factory letterhead; in the Moser factory records, the form Meyers Neffe is used.

the time de Carro settled in Karlsbad in 1826, his intensive cultural, organizational and scientific activities permeated all aspects of its social life.

In an effort to infuse the latest scientific developments into the thinking of the spa's physicians, de Carro extensively studied contemporary therapeutic procedures and, as a result, published several books dealing with new and modern methods of spa treatment. These books, translated into several languages, found world-wide acceptance and brought a flood of patrons from as far away as the Near East, India and the United States. In addition to his scientific endeavors, de Carro initiated reforms among the hotel and boardinghouse proprietors to improve guest accommodations. He also became deeply involved in the spa's cultural activities. History, literature, music and art formed a common basis upon which many long-lasting and influential acquaintances were established. To further publicize spa activities, de Carro annually published (in French) the *Karlsbad Almanac* which provided information about upcoming events for the spa season. Jean de Carro's almost superhuman efforts to transform Karlsbad into the foremost European spa resort were only terminated by his death on March 12, 1857.

At the same time that Karlsbad was developing as a spa, its porcelain and stoneware industries were becoming prominent. Production of luxury porcelain and stoneware items was supported by the existence of local supplies of high grade kaolin and ornamental stone; coal was readily available from the Falkenau basin, located several kilometers west of Karlsbad. During the off-season, Karlsbad was a typical mid-19th-century industrial town. In June and July, when the spa season was at its height, Karlsbad assumed a facade consistent with the presence of wealth and nobility.

Glass cutters and engravers began settling in Karlsbad during the first half of the 18th century. Of these men, only the name Bartholomew Teller has been recorded. In this early period, artistic endeavors rarely exceeded the decoration of spa drinking cups. Somewhat later, J. M. Tellner and his son J. O. Tellner rose to prominence. J. O. Tellner is credited with the actual founding of the Karlsbad engraving and cutting craft and was the teacher of the most famous of all Karlsbad engravers, Andreas Vincenz Peter Mattoni (signed articles bear the signature A. H. Mattoni).

Mattoni (1779-1864), a native of Karlsbad, was an exceptionally talented engraver, painter, designer and teacher. Goethe, for example, was numbered among his many customers and admirers. Numerous engraved and decorated cups, beakers and vases, designed and executed by Mattoni, presently exist; several are on display in the Karlovy Vary Museum. In addition to his artistic output, there was a rather large group of glass decorators whose professional genealogy can be traced to the tutorial expertise of this unique individual.*

Perhaps the most outstanding of Mattoni's pupils was Anton Pfeiffer (1801-1866). It is said that Pfeiffer's artistic standards surpassed even those of Mattoni. Pfeiffer successfully established a workshop in Karlsbad which employed 15 engravers, five glass blowers and five glass painters; religious as well as popular spa themes were emphasized. After his death, Pfeiffer's two brothers, Josef and Jan, carried on in the family tradition. Among Mattoni's other pupils were Rudolf Hiller (1827-1915), who was the first to open a promotional glass showroom in Karlsbad in 1853, and Anton Rudolf Dewitte (1824-1900), a noted engraver of hunting motifs who used decorative styles based on the work of Jakob Gauermann (1773-1845).

Cast before this impressive array of wealth, influence and artistic accomplishments, the birth of Ludwig Moser (1833-1916) heralded the rise of Karlsbad to even greater heights. Born in Karlsbad on June 18, 1833, Ludwig was the son of Lazar Moser, who, in 1820 was the first Jew in Karlsbad to be granted trade and traveling papers. After attending elementary school in Karlsbad, Ludwig Moser completed four years of high school taught by the Piarists (a Catholic monastic order) in Vienna. He returned to Karlsbad in 1847 to finish his high school education. In 1847 he became an apprentice to engraver Andreas Mattoni while simultaneously taking painting classes

---

*Anton Urban (1845-1909) was a pupil of Anton Pfeiffer; his elder brother Joseph Urban (died 1895), was a pupil of Mattoni. Anton Urban taught Jindrich Pfeiffer (born 1866) who was the last of the family line. Both Urban brothers are noted for their engraved spa themes, coats of arms and hunting motifs. Their descendants continued the art of engraving into the 20th century with Julius Urban (born 1883) being the last independent engraver in Karlsbad. Jindřich Boltz and Eduard Löw are also recorded as being pupils of Mattoni.

from the painter Ernst Anton; this phase of his education continued until 1850.

According to Ludwig Moser's travel log, a type of travel passport issued on October 9, 1850 (this log was retained by the Moser family but was lost during the Nazi takeover in 1938), family financial considerations forced Ludwig to seek work outside of Karlsbad. Ludwig journeyed to Prague in October of 1850, but was unable to acquire a satisfactory position. He continued on to the Grossmann Glass Cutting Company in Polish Kirchen, but there also no situation as an engraver was to be found. Disappointed, Ludwig returned on foot to Prague. In December of 1850, he returned to Karlsbad where he again served as an engraver apprentice to Mattoni.

After a short period Ludwig again traveled to Prague, this time to study painting under the supervision of the director of the Prague Art Academy, a Herr Ruben. To support his studies, Ludwig worked as an engraver at the Wilhelm Hoffman Glass Company, "Am Graben" ("On the Ditch"), for a Herr Eberl. In 1853 he returned to Karlsbad to work for the glass engraver A. H. Pfeiffer, but low pay and pressing family responsibilities forced him to travel to Germany in 1854 in search of a better position. Ludwig traveled from Zwickau to Leipzig, without success, and thence on to Berlin where he found work in an engraving shop in the Markgrafenstrasse (Land Dukes Street). During his seven-month stay in Berlin, Ludwig joined the workers' union and gained considerable recognition as an engraver of hunting and ornamental motifs.

Upon his return to Karlsbad from Berlin in 1855, Ludwig rented a "boutique" from Mattoni on the "Alten Wiesen" ("Old Meadow") near the Hotel Pupp. During the summer months, he engraved monograms, writings, seals and ornaments on drinking cups and other glass items and, on occasion, on semi-precious stones.

When the spa season was over, he worked for his parents at their home in the house "Zwei Prinzen" ("Two Princes"). In the latter part of the 1850's, Ludwig married a local Karlsbad girl. Of the six children born to the couple, only the sons Rudolf (1860-1908), Friedrich (born 1863) and Oskar (born 1864) lived long enough to become involved in the evolution of the glassworks which their father would found.

Although Ludwig Moser studied painting and engraving and was known as an accomplished artist in his own right, the world-renowned legacy of this man was not related to his artistic works, but rather to the founding and direction of a glass manufacturing firm dedicated to the perfection of artistic glass. Well aware of Jean de Carro's former successes, Ludwig also possessed exceptional organizational abilities and a keen commercial sense. He was, without question, an entrepreneur of the first rank. In his 24th year (1857), Ludwig cast aside the trappings of an isolated engraving studio and, in the manner of Rudolf Hiller and A.H. Pfeiffer, embarked on the establishment of a series of glass showrooms supported by a highly talented staff of designers, enamelists and engravers.

CHAPTER I, Selected References:
Hájek, Jindřich, "Karlovy Vary — The "Cradle of the 'Glass of Kings,'" *Czech. Glass Review,* Vol. 2 (1964) p. 42. Weiss, Gustav, *The Book of Glass,* Praeger Publishing Co., 1971. The Corning Museum of Glass, *Czechoslovakian Glass,* New York: Dover Publications, 1981. Biographical information on the life of Ludwig Moser was obtained largely from records brought to this country by Leo Moser and retained by the Corning Museum of Glass.

II. LUDWIG MOSER – GLASS DECORATOR AND ENTREPRENEUR (1857-1893)

In March of 1857 Ludwig Moser paid 65 guilden for a former restaurant which he converted into a well-equipped engraving studio. This studio was located in the Marktbrunnen Strasse (Market Fountain Street) near the sanatorium promenade in Karlsbad. He was subsequently granted a license to decorate and sell glass products in the local area. Within a relatively short period of time, the growing demand for his engravings and stone cuttings resulted in the opening of several new shops within the immediate vicinity. In spite of these early successes, 36 years would pass before Ludwig would be granted the right to melt his own glass. During those years, Moser hired talented artists from the regions surrounding Karlsbad and Steinschönau (Kamenický Šenov). In the process, he created a progressive and commercially successful business which attracted the patronage of royal houses throughout Europe. In addition, his merchandising acumen led to the development of a world-wide trade network which, in combination with unique products of the highest possible quality, brought him international recognition.

Commercial success in glass merchandising depends largely on establishing clientele with artistic appreciation as well as the means to purchase the goods proffered. With this in mind, Ludwig opened multiple commercial outlets in the most socially influential sections of Karlsbad. Moser's first retail shop was located in the spa institution known as "Umesta Výmura" ("By the Town of Weimer"). He opened a second shop in 1862 in the spa institution "Uzlatého Klíĉe" ("The Golden Key") and, in 1865, a third shop in the house known as "U ĉerveného srdce" ("The Red Heart"). This latter shop offered the most elaborate salesroom in Karlsbad and was strategically located on the main street (known as the "Old Meadow") of the spa quarter. For his own paintings and designs, Moser purchased raw glass from the best south Bohemian glass blowing companies—Meyr's Neffe (in Winterberg), Wilhelm Kralik

(Eleonorenhain) and Loetz Witwe (Kostermuehle); light fixtures to be decorated were purchased from Pallme at Steinschönau in northern Bohemia. During this period the ranks of the fledgling Moser firm swelled to encompass several dozen local workers.

Fig. 1 Engraved covered goblet entitled "Gretchen Accompanied by Faust". Executed by Johann F. Hoffman, Karlsbad, after 1882. Unsigned. Compliments of the Prague Museum of Decorative Arts (inventory no. 74.465).

In response to the increased product demand which accompanied his marketing expansion, Ludwig Moser opened a new decorating workshop in Meistersdorf* near Steinschönau in northern Bohemia. This facility, organized around 1870, included engraving and cutting shops and a large enameling studio under the direction of a Herr Kneipe. From its inception, the Moser firm employed only the finest engravers, cutters and enamelists. With the opening of the Meistersdorf facility, these highly skilled artists and artisans were primarily recruited from the north Bohemian region of Haida (Nový Bor) and Steinschönau. As might be expected, many of the artistic styles indigenous to this area of Bohemia were strongly reflected in the glassware produced by the Moser firm during the 1870-1893 period.

Sparse records have yielded the names of only a few of the most prominent designers/engravers who worked for the Moser firm during this early period. No names of enamelists remain. Among Moser's employees were Eduard Hoffman (died 1878) and his son Johann (1842-1900). These men were exceptionally talented engravers who specialized in figural motifs. In addition to the example in Figure 1, further references to the work of Johann Hoffman may be found in Corning's *Czechoslovakian Glass* and *Glas des Historismus* by Walter Spiegl. It is recorded that Ludwig Lobmeyr (then acting director of the Viennese based glasshouse of J.&L. Lobmeyr), upon observation of the engraved glass sent by Johann Hoffman to the 1873 Vienna Exhibition, commented that although Hoffman's work did not always adhere to accepted compositional guidelines, his engraving technique satisfied the highest expectations.

Emanuel Hoffman, a portrait engraver of considerable importance, and his son Jan worked for Moser for many years. Additional names include Josef Urban and Rudolf Hiller, both of whom were students of Andreas Mattoni; their respective sons; and the artists/engravers Sacher, Dietl and Nowak (known for his figurals and ornamental decorations). At the 1873 Vienna World Exhibition, Moser's display featured chalices engraved by Wilhelm van Kaulback (1805-1874) and Friedrich Gauermann (1807-1862).

Due to their geographical proximity, much of the raw glass consumed by the Meistersdorf branch was probably purchased from factories around Haida and Steinschönau; Emanuel Hoffman is said to have obtained most of his glass blanks from Graf Harrach (Nový Svêt).

By 1873, Moser was managing five individual shops, the Meistersdorf refinery (which employed some 56 workers) and sales outlets in St. Petersburg, New York, Paris and London. In that same year, the glass shop, cutting and engraving workshops, and the inventory of the Imperial and Royal Privileged "Burgstein" Mirror Factory at Röhrsdorf (Sloup) came under his control. After 1874, Moser's expansion and commercial thrusts were overshadowed by his desire to obtain permission to build his own glassworks at Karlsbad. Nearly 20 frustrating years were spent fighting the corrupt and anti-Semitic Austrian bureaucracy before his dream was finally realized.

Initially, Moser merchandised not only his own glass products but also those of other glass decorators in the Karlsbad area. As Moser's dominance in the market place increased, however, many of these decorators found it necessary to merge with the Moser firm to secure a continuing outlet for their artistic endeavors. Advertisements from the period attest to the wide assortment of glassware sold. Included were mirrors and a large selection of tableware in fine Muslin* glass and in cut crystal. Moser's products often adhered to the tradition of engraved or gilded monograms and emblems, or of engraved hunting scenes, but also offered more intricate and artistically challenging compositions. Of primary importance to the identification of glassware produced during this period was the consensus of contemporary experts that decorative glass marketed by Moser in the Karlsbad region exhibited artistic characteristics which were unique. Consequently, one concludes that the majority of artistic glass, identified to be of Moser origin, did not have counterparts produced by other Central European glasshouses.

Ludwig Moser ranks as a pioneer of the modern glass industry which began to develop in Bohemia

---

*Meistersdorf was known as the Village of Masters and was the source of many of the finest artists and engravers to emerge from Bohemia. (ref. Alfred S. Johnston, *The Fritsche Ewer*, New York, 1886)

Muslin Glass: In the early days, Muslin glass was produced by overlaying glass with wax-soaked lace material and submerging the combination in an acid bath. The resulting pattern had the appearance of fine muslin cloth.

in the middle of the 19th century. During this period, the Bohemian glass industry, based on the ever-improving technology associated with the Industrial Revolution, as well as on progressive management and marketing techniques, was developing the ability to succeed in the highly competitive international trade arena of the future. Artistic ideas originating in England also began to influence Bohemia. These ideas were concerned with the function of art and the manner in which it could be used to enhance human environments. Moser used these concepts, but in reverse—he created environments which would enhance the value of the artistic glass he sold. Moser's salesrooms were effective not only from an aesthetic standpoint, but also from a commercial one. They represented an early embodiment of the idea that artistically fine items placed in the correct environment will sell themselves.

In addition to selling in shops during the relatively short-lived spa season, Moser became heavily involved in exhibitions and artistic auctions. A letter preserved in the Karlovy Vary Museum, written to Moser by the director of the Museum of Art and Industry in Vienna and dated January 14, 1869 states:

> *"Mr. Ludwig Moser, industrial glass-maker of Karlsbad, has several times exhibited articles of crystal glass in this museum which where outstanding for their technical perfection of cut."*

At the 1873 Vienna World Exhibition, the exhibits which featured the work of Moser engravers Wilhelm van Kaulbach and Friedrich Gauermann resulted in Moser's being awarded a Medal for Merits. As a result of subsequent sales, Moser shortly thereafter acquired the enviable distinction of being appointed supplier to the Austrian Imperial Court of Franz Joseph.

Moser also exhibited at the 1878 Paris International Exposition where he displayed enameled and gilded glass decorated in Islamic and Japanese motifs. A noted contemporary French art critic, who was known to comment favorably only on French art, complimented Moser's efforts to effect a significant change in Bohemian artistic glass form. It is recorded in an advertisement in *A Guide to Karlsbad,* published in 1880 and written by Dr. E. Hlaváček, that Moser products had received many honorable prizes at various exhibitions. Specific information regarding the dates and locations of most of these exhibitions is unknown to the authors; however, there is little doubt that Moser was rapidly becoming one of the foremost artistic glass suppliers in Central Europe. The growing influence of the Moser firm was reflected in the appointment of Ludwig Moser as a member of the jury (in this context, juries were responsible for the judging at glass competitions) for the Austro-Hungarian confederation at the 1889 World Exhibition in Paris. Participation in shows in Glasgow and Edinburgh resulted in Moser's appointment to the glass jury for these areas.

In contrast to the laurels being garnered in Europe, Moser's marketing efforts in New York were apparently beset by numerous difficulties. As recorded in an 1887 trade journal, excessive appraisals by customs agents, low product demand and high costs associated with maintaining a New York showroom forced the sales representative, Rudolph Moser, to terminate operations. In 1891, a new outlet was established by Rudolf's brother Oskar at No. 23 Union Square. After

Fig. 2   Left to right, Gustov, Leo, Richard and Carl Moser.

five years of operation, this shop was forced to close, with all remaining stock being turned over for public auction.

After the death of his first wife, Ludwig married Julie Meyer (of the Meyer glassmaking family) around 1875. This union was blessed by the birth of four sons: Carl, Gustav, Leo (1879-1974) and Richard. Carl Moser was educated as a doctor and did not become involved in the glassmaking industry. Gustav later moved to Paris where, for many years, he managed the Moser factory outlet on the Boulevard des Italiens. From the early 20th century on, Leo and Richard served the Moser firm in various capacities, finally becoming the firm's artistic and commercial directors, respectively.

A major flood in the late fall of 1891 caused extensive damage to the residential, resort and commercial areas in Karlsbad. Out of this devastation grew a new and modernized city—and for Ludwig Moser, a larger display room in the "Roten Herz."

Increased sales, persistent difficulties associated with acquiring suitable raw glass, and the extreme distance to the Meistersdorf refinery (85-100 miles) brought about a renewed effort to obtain approval to construct a modern glass manufacturing company and refinery in the town of Meierhöfen, only three kilometers from Karlsbad.* On June 4, 1892, the Ministry of the Interior in Vienna finally granted the Moser firm permission to build glass furnaces in the Karlsbad area.

---

*In Central European terminology, a glass refinery is responsible for the decoration of glass, not the melting and forming of glass blanks.

CHAPTER II, Selected References:

Hájek, Jindřich, "Karlovy Vary—The Cradle of the 'Glass of Kings,'" *Czech. Glass Review,* Vol. 2 (1964), p. 42. The years 1857-1893 represent a period in Moser history about which little has been written. Much of the information contained in this chapter, particularly with respect to Moser's Meistersdorf facility, was derived from records brought to this country by Leo Moser and retained by the Corning Museum of Glass.

III. MOSER AT MEIERHÖFEN— A DREAM FULFILLED (1893-1938)

1893 marked the opening of Ludwig Moser's new glass fabrication and decorating facility in Meierhöfen. Organized by Moser and his three sons, Rudolf, Oskar and Friedrich, under the name "Karlsbader Glas-industrie Gesellschaft Ludwig Moser & Söhne, A. G. Meierhöfen bei Karlsbad," this undertaking not only represented the long-awaited fulfillment of Ludwig Moser's dreams, but also the foundation for one of the most technically innovative and artistically precise sources of fine glass the world has ever known. The entire management of the Moser firm was moved to Meierhöfen, and the new facility was staffed with the foremost glassmakers and cutters available in Bohemia. These glass artisans, partially attracted by the offer of free modern housing and heating, were primarily recruited from the Sumava mountain region in southern Bohemia. Richard Kralik was appointed works foreman and chief melter; Rudolf Novak was foreman of the cutting workshop.* Both of these men came from Meyr's Neffe's Adolf glassworks at Winterberg and were renowned for their expertise in the production of high quality Bohemian crystal. Attached to the main glass factory was an extensive glass decorating studio which employed the region's finest artists and designers.

An interesting postscript to the opening of the Meierhöfen works is provided by the testimony of a retired glass blower who worked for the Moser firm for over 30 years. According to this account, recorded in the March 1960 issue of the East German periodical *Weltbuehne,* 1895 was the earliest date at which the glass-melting furnaces became operational. At that time the first in a series of financial crises hit the Moser firm. In his preoccupation with constructing a glassworks of uncompromising capability, Ludwig Moser had simply run out of money. Ludwig called his workers together, apprised them of the situation, and entreated them to remain until business improved.

*Richard Kralik (b. 1852) was the son of Wilhelm Kralik and Louise Lobmeyr and was a noted poet, musician, philosopher and historian.

This the workers agreed to do, despite the fact that there was apparently a considerable delay before they once again received compensation for their efforts.

An important glass type, one which contained a large proportion of chalk (calcium carbonate) in combination with potash (potassium carbonate), was first produced in Bohemia about 1680. Because of its improved clarity and hard brilliance when cut, this new glass, alternately referred to as "chalk glass" or "Bohemian crystal," formed the basis upon which the early Bohemian cut and engraved glass industry flourished. Although chalk glass represented a significant advancement over the prior glassmaking art, it did not possess the refractive properties and high level of transparency characteristic of the lead crystal developed by Ravenscroft in England. Through the years, numerous attempts were made to develop a glass which would combine the desirable properties of lead crystal with the rock-crystal-like characteristics of chalk glass. One of the most successful of these endeavors was a soda (sodium hydroxide)-potash glass manufactured by the Meyr's Neffe's Adolf glassworks.

As a testament to the quality and commercial acceptance of Bohemian crystal, Leo Moser, in an article titled "Commercial Art Glass," which appeared in the March 1942 issue of *The Glass Industry,* stated that "No lead crystal had been produced in Central Europe prior to 1914; all lead crystal had been imported into Central Europe from the U.S., England, France and Belgium." Moser goes on to state that after 1919, Bohemian production of lead crystal increased to the point of reducing imported quantities to the near-zero level. Although Moser produced limited amounts of lead crystal after 1919, various forms of Bohemian crystal dominated production up until the onset of World War II. In addition to the traditional Bohemian crystal, the Moser firm introduced a series of new glass colors in deep rich shades after 1895. These new colors initially added a distinctive ingredient to engraved Art Nouveau glass while,

Fig. 3 Moser factory at Meierhöfen.

in the long term, they represented the foundation upon which the majority of artistic glass produced at Meierhöfen was based.

Concurrent with the firing of the glass furnaces at Meierhöfen came the search for perfection in the manufactured quality of glass. Samples which were judged inferior by Moser's shop supervisors were immediately destroyed. Quality control of this severity, similar to that practiced at the Steuben Glass Works, resulted in a well-deserved reputation for producing crystal glass unsurpassed by any contemporary manufacturer. Deeply engraved Art Nouveau and Modern style glass are just two of many examples which bear witness to the success of this philosophy. Even before the advent of World War I, examples of Moser glass were among the most valued possessions of world rulers, wealthy personages, statesmen and diplomats. Mass production techniques were never employed at the Moser glassworks. Each piece of glass produced represented an original and unique artistic achievement.

Initially, glass products marketed by the Moser firm included wine sets, tableware, vases, bowls, jardinieres, jewel and ash trays, spa cups and other decorative glass. Most of these items could be obtained as unadorned crystal, engraved and/or gilded, or with enameled embellishments. As it was prior to 1893, custom work for important clientele remained a growing and ever-important segment of Moser pro-

duction. With the passage of time, the selection of shapes and decorative styles was constantly expanded. The composition of drinking and table sets grew to encompass new types of stemware and tumblers designed specifically for various wines, liqueurs and cognacs; slender champagne goblets; beer tankards; glasses for water and other beverages; finger bowls; fruit and sweet-meat bowls; jugs and decanters. In consort with this exceptional selection of tableware was the world famous Moser banquet table set which became the cherished possession of world rulers and other important people; these sets typically bore engraved monograms or other decorations highlighted with 24K gold.

After the Moser firm recovered from its initial financial difficulties, its business opportunities increased at a heady pace. Due in part to sponsored shows, ranging from Cairo to Bombay to New York, Ludwig Moser recognized that a world-wide network of commercial outlets was required to ensure the sale of his company's products. The Brussels World Exhibition in 1897, at which Ludwig was vice president of the glass jury, proved financially quite successful for the firm. In the summer of 1897, Ludwig decided to establish a new shop in Paris. It opened in October of that year under the management of his son Gustav. Located in the "Maison Doree" on the Boulevard des Italiens, Moser's Paris outlet exists to the present day. A steady increase in the volume of spa clientele, as well as a highly acclaimed participation in the 1900 World Exhibition in Paris, skyrocketed the name of Moser glass into international prominence.

An insight into the production capability of the Moser firm during this period is provided by a listing of facilities in the *Austria-Hungary Glass Industry* index for the year 1910. The Meierhöfen plant is recorded as having two melting ovens with 20 open ports (four with caps) fired by a brown-coal Siebert system, 88 steam-driven cutting workbenches and painting, engraving, etching and printing departments. A total of 400 employees produced a yearly output of 6,000 metric tons. Workers in front of the ovens typically labored under what were termed "Austrian patriotic conditions"—12-hour shifts and no vacation or insurance benefits.

As a good businessman, Moser knew that appreciation of fine glass is rarely spontaneous, but that, rather, it grows with an exposure to the whole artistic and technical process of glassmaking. With this in mind, the Moser firm allowed clients to witness the making of glass from "working of the melt" to the finished product in on-site sales rooms. (This technique is still being employed by the Steuben Glass Works in Corning, N.Y.) Personalities so honored included King Edward VII of England, the Shah of Persia, the King of Siam and the Maharajahs of Hyderabad and Travancore. Edward VII was sufficiently impressed with the quality of Moser glass that he ordered a complete set of tableware, now known as the "Royal" set (Plate 151). This set was later duplicated for Edward's wife, Queen Alexandra, and for King Haakon VII of Norway and Turkish Sultan Abdul Hamid. According to a 1964 article in the *Czech Glass Review,* the "Royal" set, in a somewhat modernized version, is still being used on official occasions by all Czechoslovakian embassies and diplomatic missions. Moser also organized a tour service which, in cooperation with the hotel and spa institutions located in Karlsbad, was designed to alleviate the boredom of wealthy potential clientele. These tours, with a stop in luxurious sample rooms from which articles could be purchased, succeeded in introducing the world of glassmaking to an otherwise disinterested segment of society.

The Moser firm's further expansion at home and abroad was initiated by the opening in 1903 of a sales outlet in the house known as "Berliner Hof" on Kaiserstrasse in Marienbad (Mariánské Lázně). In 1905, sales outlets were realized in the Palace Hotel in Franzenbad (Františkovy Lázně) and the "Galleria Vittorio Emmanuele" in Milano. An additional shop was opened in Teplitz and, finally, a large and important sales outlet was established in Prague. Foreign sales were supported by branch offices, such as on the Boulevard des Italiens in Paris and in Bombay, India, which were staffed either by members of the Moser family or by other experienced personnel. A factory training program was instituted by the Moser firm to develop sales personnel with expertise in the closely related fields of artistic glass and porcelain. These people were responsible for placing Moser products in independently owned shops in the spa areas and in stores throughout the world known to specialize in quality artistic items.

As indicated by the listing at the end of this chapter, participation in international shows continued with an important showing at the World Exhibition in St. Louis in 1904. On January 25, 1908, the Moser firm was appointed "Glass Manufacturers at Karlsbad" to his Majesty Edward VII of England; this prestigious title was renewed after the King's death in 1911. Moser's penetration of world markets in combination with an unwavering dedication to excellence had earned for Moser glass the enviable title of the "Glass of Kings."

One is inclined to stop and speculate on the reason for training sales personnel to be experts in the dual fields of glass and porcelain. As early as 1870 Ludwig Moser had established strong commercial and artistic ties with the Teplitz Cermaic Art School. This relationship dealt primarily with design development, and we have been unable to uncover any additional references which define any specific involvement of the Moser firm with the manufacture, decoration, or marketing of porcelain products. Karlsbad and its environs were noted for the production of fine quality porcelain and these products were undoubtedly marketed by Ludwig Moser during the formative years of his firm. In particular, the Epiag china factory in Karlsbad, which was owned and managed by another branch of the Moser family, produced high quality porcelain products well into the 1930's. Due to the extensive differences in the manufacturing techniques required to produce and decorate glass and porcelain, it is unlikely that the Moser glass factory would have engaged in the processing of porcelain products. Considering the extensive network of worldwide outlets established by Ludwig Moser, however, it does seem probable that the Moser firm marketed the porcelain products of selected manufacturers as an adjunct to their own output of artistic glass.

A reorganization of the Moser firm, which occurred around 1900, left son Rudolf Moser as the acting director. About this time, specific references regarding Ludwig Moser disappear from the available literature. One suspects that Ludwig, by then 67, preferred to turn over a major portion of the company management to his younger and more energetic sons. Considering his intimate involvement with glassmaking, Ludwig most likely remained in the background in the capacity of controlling interest and technical consultant until his death on September 27, 1916. Evidence suggests that when Rudolf died in 1908, Leo Moser assumed the duties of commercial director for a short period of time. In 1916, Richard Moser became the commercial director and Leo the artistic director.

As World War I began in the summer of 1914, Moser production was dramatically reduced. Loss of spa clientele, the drafting of many into the military, the severence of commercial ties to related industries and the loss of lucrative foreign markets were responsible for this decline. An extremely important characteristic of a hand-processed industry is its ability to adapt to rapidly changing artistic styles or market requirements with a minimum loss in time and money. At no other point in history was this ability more important to the survival of the Moser firm. Under the direction of Leo Moser, product lines previously designed to fit the specialized requirements of various side branches were modified to be compatible with whatever export or internal markets could be uncovered. As an example, in 1916 Moser introduced a series of cups which imitated in the finest detail the glasses produced originally by Johann Mildner (1763-1808). These cups were enameled with a miniature portrait of Emperor Wilhelm II and bore the inscription "Gott mit uns, Wilhelm"; they made exellent gifts in patriotic circles. This hand-to-mouth existence proved successful, and by the spring of 1916 business began a slow upward turn.

With the capitulation of Austria-Hungary on October 28, 1918, Czechoslovakia was declared an independent state by the natonal committee in Prague. Karlsbad and Meierhöfen, once part of the rich and powerful Austro-Hungarian Empire, found themselves within the boundaries of this newly formed Czechoslovakian state. Although names and national boundaries were changed (Karlsbad assumed the name Karlovy Vary and Meierhöfen was renamed Dvory), the high quality of Moser glass remained unaltered. In fact, glass produced by the Moser firm during the following decade would reach a pinnacle of perfection and world-wide recognition unrivaled throughout the prior years of the firm's existence.

Immediately following the cessation of hostilities, the market for artistic glass increased perceptably.

Fig. 4   Leo Moser seated in his office at the Meierhöfen glassworks.

11

Although this proved to be but a brief respite before the gathering storm, it apparently instilled sufficient confidence in Richard Moser to enter into negotiations for the acquisition of several rival firms. When the value of the Kronen finally collapsed in the wake of four years of war, these negotiations were terminated, and Richard was forced to seek aid from the Bohemian Union Bank to forestall imminent bankruptcy. Controlling interest in the Moser firm was acquired by the Union Bank who assumed full financial responsibility; Richard and Leo were retained on the board of directors. Even though the management of Ludwig Moser and Söhne had now passed irretrievably out of family hands, Leo Moser, as artistic director, continued to exert a dramatic influence over the firm's output of artistic glass. Richard Moser, being largely relieved of the financial burdens normally associated with his post as commercial director, was free to cultivate the friendship of influential people and expand the visibility of the Moser firm through its representation at important international expositions.

In 1922, the Moser firm merged with the Meyr's Neffe Adolf glassworks at Winterberg (Vimperk) to form a limited company by the rather lengthy name of "The Karlsbad Factory for Crystal Glass Ltd. Co. Ludwig Moser and Sons and Meyer's Nephews."* With the acquisition of the Adolf works, the total

Moser plant was increased to include six glass ovens with 68 ports, 248 cutting workbenches, an additional engraving and painting department, and 750 workers. According to the 1925 edition of the *Address Book of the European Glass Industry* (published by the magazine *The Glass Huette)* a Herr Benno Hess was named acting director of the Adolf works. Moser's merger with Meyr's Neffe not only dramatically increased capacity for producing artistic glass, but considerably increased Moser's access to the cumulative design capacity of the Wiener Werkstätte association of artists.

In light of the significant artistic influence which the Wiener Werkstätte was destined to exert on Moser production, it would seem appropriate to digress a few moments and present a historical synopsis of this internationally acclaimed design organization. As a response to the freedom of the Art Nouveau movement sweeping Europe, a group of Viennese painters, sculptors and architects in 1897 formed an association known as the Vienna Secession. Koloman Moser (born in Vienna in 1868, died in 1918)* and Josef Olbrich (1867-1908), charter members of the Vienna Secession, were commissioned by E. Bakalowitz Söhn of Vienna to design decorative vases and tableware; these designs, in turn, were produced by several Bohemian glasshouses, including Meyr's Neffe. In 1900, Koloman Moser and Josef Hoffman (1870-1956) organized the VIIIth Secession (Art Nouveau) Exhibition to which, among others, had been invited Charles Rennie Mackintosh and his wife, Margaret Macdonald, and Charles Robert Ashbee and his Guild of Handicrafts. On a subsequent visit to Scotland and London, Moser was sufficiently impressed with the workshop system developed by Ashbee that he returned to Austria consumed with the idea of developing a similar organization. In May of 1903, Moser and Hoffman succeeded in obtaining the financial backing of Fritz Wärndorfer, a young art collector and banker, and the Weiner Werkstätte was founded with Koloman Moser and Josef Hoffman as artistic directors. Consisting of a series of individual workshops specializing in all phases of the decorative arts, the Wiener Werkstätte was dedicated to the harmonious incorporation of design elements, both from an architectural and an

*On October 22, 1814, the government of Winterberg submitted a request to the Piseker Regional Office for permission to build a glass manufacturing and cutting facility "for the Gratzener Glassmaster Josef Meyer" (1732-1829). Built on the site of an older glassworks founded by Count Adolf of Schwarzenberg, from which the glasshouse derives its name, the financial success of this undertaking brought welcomed prosperity to Winterberg. After the death of Josef Meyer, his favorite son, Johann (1775-1841), assumed control of the Adolf glassworks. Wilhelm Kralik (1806-1877), a gifted glassmaker and trusted worker for Johann Meyer, in 1831 married Meyer's niece Anna Pinhak. Josef Taschek (1814-1862) was the son of Meyer's sister Johanna; later, Josef married Wilhelm Kralik's oldest daughter, Ferdinandea. When Johann died in 1841, Wilhelm Kralik and Josef Taschek merged the glassworks of Adolf, Eleonorenhain and Kaltenbach into the largest single firm in Bohemia, known by the name of Meyr's Neffe (Meyer's Nephews). In 1854, Meyr's Neffe acquired the glass holloware factories of Ernstbrunn and Franzensthal. At a later date, Idathal and Louisenhütte, located in close proximity to the Adolf works, were also purchased. After Josef Taschek's death, Wilhelm Kralik managed the entire Meyr's Neffe complex. At this time, Meyr's Neffe was known as one of the foremost Bohemian producers of high quality glass products. This reputation, in addition to the marriage between the daughter of Josef Lobmyer, Louise, and Wilhelm Kralik in 1851, prompted Ludwig Lobmeyr to entrust Meyr's Neffe with the production of a new style of Renaissance-type glassware in the late 1860's; this close and profitable relationship between J. & L. Lobmeyr and Meyr's Neffe was maintained for many years. Approximately four years after Wilhelm Kralik's death in 1881, the original firm of Meyr's Neffe was subdivided among his four sons; Karl and Hugo Kralik (died 1883) retained the glassworks at Winterberg (Adolf), Idathal and Louisenhütte, as well as the name of Meyr's Neffe. After Karl Kralik's death, his sons Rudolf and Albert became co-owners of Meyr's Neffe.

*Our research has uncovered no direct relationship between Ludwig and Koloman Moser.

interior décor point of view. Koloman Moser, apparently restless in his search for artistic ideals, left the Wiener Werkstätte in 1906 to join a splinter group led by the painter Gustav Klint. From this point until his death in 1918, Koloman Moser's professional career remains shrouded in obscurity. Although Moser's departure had a significant impact on the design capability of the Wiener Werkstätte, new and talented artists continued to join and the organization flourished.

After World War I, the Moser firm became recognized as the foremost Bohemian producer of artistic glass and luxury tableware. Perfection in the glass medium and forming techniques, coupled with the work of highly skilled specialists in the fields of cutting and engraving, resulted in a flood of individual production orders intended primarily for exhibition purposes. In this regard, Moser executed designs for the professors and pupils of the School of Applied Art in Prague for exhibition at the 1925 International Exhibition of Decorative Arts in Paris. One of these pupils, Hana Dostálová, exhibited a magnificently cut and engraved jardiniére which later won a prize in another Parisian competition. Engravings produced by Hana Dostálová are now sought by discriminating art collectors all over the world. Another pupil, Ludvika Smrêková, destined to become one of the most famous Czechoslovakian artists, submitted designs which, according to one reference, were never realized in glass form. Chris Lebeau, a noted Dutch graphic artist and designer, was responsible for the production of large quantities of Unikati ("one-of-a-kind") while a visitor at the Moser factory from 1926 to 1929. Characterized by the sensual melding of form, color and texture accented by the use of rim edging in contrasting colors, Lebeau's work represents a significant departure from the more classical Moser styles.

Fig. 5   Leo Moser in the Vatican for the presentation of the Pope's drinking service.

13

Glass produced by the Moser firm for the Wiener Werkstätte emphasized richly colored glass shaped with cut facets. This style enjoyed considerable popularity during the 1920's and falls under the general category of Fantazie Moser. Cubistic Art Deco forms were produced for more than a decade. Moser continued the long established tradition of enameled glass decoration, which permitted participation in the exhibition of painted glass held at the Arts and Crafts Museum in Prague in 1924. In response to Moser's display of decorated glass at this exhibition, Prague art critic Karel Herain wrote:

"The products of the Moser glasswork are first class both artistically and technically. They penetrate into the elegant strata and adapt themselves to this task with refined taste and a sense for originality. The glassworks can be regarded as an exemplary enterprise, especially due to its co-operation with artists, founded on a specialized basis. The prosperity of the works proves the error of the opinion that Czech glassworks should base their production merely on the demands of the consumer."

Early in the 1920's, Moser was the first glasshouse to introduce a new line of colored glasses based entirely on rare-earth oxide colorants. Developed, in part, by Leo Moser, these exotic glasses exhibit dichroic-like characteristics (in the sense of dual colors; perceived color is a function of glass thickness and background illumination). Uniquely suited to the established Modern and Art Deco cutting styles, products featuring these new glasses were awarded a gold medal at the 1925 International Exhibition of Decorative Arts in Paris.

In 1923, Leo Moser presented a 218-piece crystal drinking tableservice for 24 persons to Pope Pius XI. Each piece was finely engraved with the pontifical tiara. Cost was no object in achieving the highest possible quality; so delicate and exacting was this task that only four engravers in the entire factory were entrusted with its execution. In response to this presentation and the accompanying social reception, the following letter of appreciation was drafted at the Vatican and sent to the Moser factory:

Staatssekretariat   From the Vatican
S. H.   May 28, 1923
Nr. 18.315
Your Honorable!
    You are probably well aware after the personal reception accorded you, the degree of pleasure with which His Holiness has received your artistically executed Crystal Table Service. The rare quality of engraving exhibited by this expensive gift evokes the admiration of His Holiness and gives the Holy Father reason for undivided and hearty praise.
    The Holy Father would like to express a wish that you forward his feeling and admiration to all the other men of the famous Karlsbad Crystal Company that worked together with your honorable. His lively wish is also that his words of appreciation and thanks be conveyed to the hard-working workers that created this expensive work with artistic talent and exactness.
    In as much as I forward to you the expressed wishes from the Holy Father, I also part with my expression of exceptional and high admiration.
Your Honorable bowing,
V. D. Gaspari, m.p.
The Honorable
Mr. Leo Moser

International publicity surrounding this presentation produced a flood of orders for duplicate sets. However, requested prices by potential customers were well below initial production costs. After much deliberation and an intensive analysis of production techniques, Leo Moser set up a production line in which several engravers were each given a tool designed to do a simple but specific task. Results of this innovation surpassed expectations and the rate of production was increased three-fold without a significant loss in quality. Demand remained sufficiently high that 30 men were occupied full time filling orders for the "Pope's" set.

As noted earlier, over the years Moser glass became internationally known as the "Glass of Kings." While to some this title may seem somewhat pretentious, the list of wealthy and important people known to have purchased Moser glass is lengthy indeed. Moser was named supplier to the Royal House of Hapsburg and the King of England, and its customers included such notables as Edward VII of England, Queen Alexandra and Queen Elizabeth of England,

Fig. 6   Moser advertising sample of their most famous tableservices.

Fig. 7   Maria Theresa engraved dinner set no. 10620. Produced by the Moser Glassworks throughout a major portion of the first half of the 20th century. Compliments of the Prague Museum of Decorative Arts.

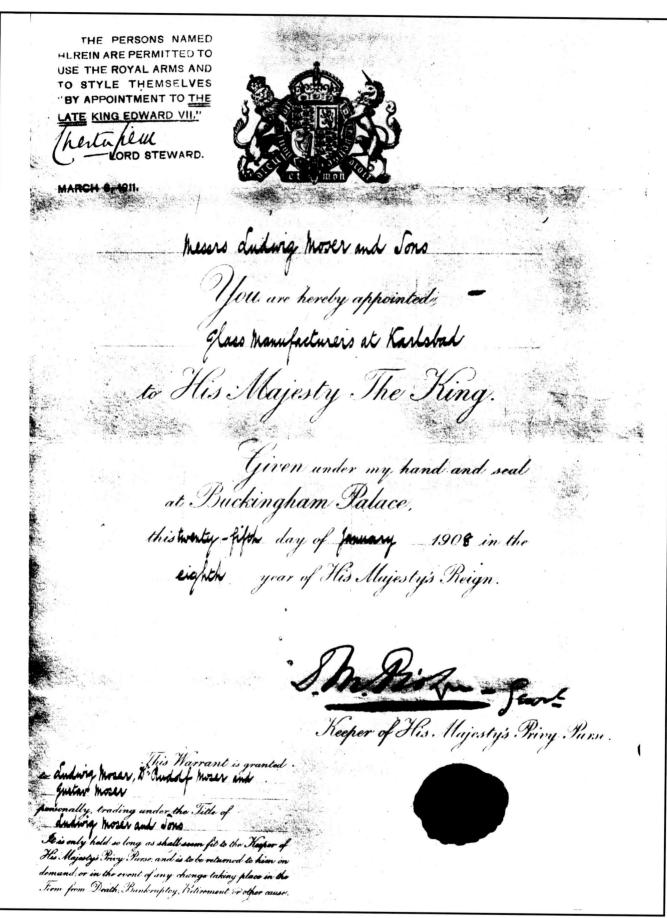

THE PERSONS NAMED
HEREIN ARE PERMITTED TO
USE THE ROYAL ARMS AND
TO STYLE THEMSELVES
"BY APPOINTMENT TO THE
LATE KING EDWARD VII."

Chesterfield
LORD STEWARD.

MARCH 6, 1911.

Messrs Ludwig Moser and Sons

You are hereby appointed:

Glass Manufacturers at Karlsbad

to His Majesty The King.

Given under my hand and seal
at Buckingham Palace,
this twenty-fifth day of January 1908 in the
eighth year of His Majesty's Reign.

Keeper of His Majesty's Privy Purse.

This Warrant is granted
to Ludwig Moser, Dr Rudolf Moser and
Gustav Moser
personally, trading under the Title of
Ludwig Moser and Sons
It is only held so long as shall seem fit to the Keeper of
His Majesty's Privy Purse, and is to be returned to him on
demand, or in the event of any change taking place in the
Firm from Death, Bankruptcy, Retirement or other causes.

Fig. 8   Document of appointment as supplier of glass to the English Court of Edward VII.

Pope Pius XI, Emperor Wilhelm II of Germany, King Alphonso XIII of Spain, King Faud I of Egypt, King Zachir Mohammed Shah and King Amanullah of Afghanistan, Sultan Sidi Mohammed Ben Jussef of Morocco, King Haakon VII of Norway, King Victor Emmanuel II of Italy, Czar Boris of Bulgaria, King Carol of Rumania, Prince Regent Paul of Yugoslavia, President Inskander Mirsa of Pakistan, President Asreirsson of Iceland, Emperor Haile Selassie I of Ethiopia, Sultan Abdul Hamid of Turkey and the Shah of Persia.

Due to the high cost of acquisition and the educational level usually associated with appreciation of its finer qualities, luxury glass has a limited demand in any given geographical area. This marketing dilemma had been addressed by Ludwig Moser through his establishment of an extensive world-wide network of commercial outlets. It is not surprising, therefore, that when the Great Depression hit the United States in October of 1929, the resulting tidal wave of financial disasters which swept the world impacted heavily on the Moser firm. 1931 saw the collapse of the largest Austrian and German banks. In 1932, the Moser firm experienced severe financial difficulties which led the Bohemian Union Bank to propose that the value of stockholders' shares be reduced to 20% of their original value. A desperate attempt was made by Leo Moser to regain financial stability by introducing several new lines of low-cost art glass. Unfortunately, due to financial pressures beyond his control and the malignant environment surrounding the Nazi rise to prominence in Germany, this effort was destined to fail. In 1933 the Adolf works at Winterberg was sold. That same year witnessed the severence of the Moser family from the company founded by Ludwig Moser 76 years before; the remaining Moser brothers sold their corporate shares to the Bohemian Union Bank.

Leo Moser left Meierhöfen shortly after the brothers' corporate shares were sold. Richard, however, chose to remain with the firm for an undetermined period of time; later, he accepted a position in Prague as the resident manager of a Swiss based merchandising firm. The manifest artistic and technical contributions of Leo to the success of the Moser firm have been reasonably well recorded. Of equal importance was Richard's adroit organization of international exhibitions and his ability to move freely in the elegant strata of European society. Possessed of musical talent, Richard attended the Vienna Conservatory as a young man and was an accomplished pianist and flutist. His pleasing countenance and engaging personality won him many influential friends. Among these were the King and Queen of England, who, during the 1920's, were instrumental in the appointment of Richard as British vice consul to the spa towns of Marienbad, Franzenbad and Karlsbad. Shortly after the Sudetenland fell into Nazi hands, Richard met with his only son, Ludwig, in Prague for the last time. In a fatalistic yet prophetic statement, Richard declared his belief that Europe was lost and, after bidding farewell, left Prague for South America. Ludwig was later interned by the Nazi and spent 42 months in various concentration camps. By the time Ludwig arrived in the United States in 1948, all contact with his father had been irretrievably lost. After the war it was rumored that Richard had settled in Sao Paulo, Brazil; however, the location of Richard's adopted home in the Americas and the date of his death remain ostensibly unknown.

After his departure from Meierhöfen, Leo Moser became the managing director of several glass factories owned by the largest glass concern in Bohemia, Joseph Inwald Ltd. of Prague. These factories, located at Podebrady, Schutzendorf and Teplitz, specialized in the manufacture of hollow and cut glassware which was exported primarily to England, Australia, South America and the United States. While with Inwald, Leo introduced modernized machinery and improved manufacturing methods which substantially elevated the world-wide marketing position of the Inwald firm. Recognizing the danger Hitler represented to those of Jewish faith, Leo obtained American passports for his wife, Paolo, and son, Thomas. When his wife and son departed for the United States in June of 1938, Leo's daughter, Lea, chose to remain with her father in Europe. In August of 1938, after Hitler's bloodless annexation of Austria and before his conquest of the Sudetenland, Leo Moser and his daughter fled to France.

In France, Leo contacted his brother, Monsieur Gustav Moser, French citizen, Médaille Militaire, Croix de Guerre, who, for 42 years, had been proprietor of the Moser sales outlet in Paris at 30 Boulevard des

Fig. 9 Cut punch bowl and glasses designed by Jan Kotêra and executed by the Count Harrach Glassworks, Nový Svêt. Initially designed around 1903 with an engraved frieze but simplified after 1910. Compliments of the Prague Museum of Decorative Arts (inventory no. 14.170).

Italiens. While in Paris, and prior to his appointment as director-designer at Cristalleries de St.-Louis in early 1939, Leo was repeatedly employed as a technical consultant to several large French glasshouses. In addition to being a noted designer of cut glass, Leo Moser was intrigued by the improvement of manufacturing machinery and techniques capable of increasing productivity without sacrificing quality. These interests, coupled with extensive experience in the area of Bohemian glassmaking, were profitably employed at St.-Louis. A considerable body of dated and signed cut glass designs were generated by Leo during his tenure with this firm. Many of Leo Moser's

designs were executed and marketed by Cristalleries de St.-Louis.

Concurrent with his acceptance of a position with Cristalleries de St.-Louis, Leo and his daughter moved to the plant's location in the province of Alsace-Lorraine. There they remained until the German invasion of the Low Countries in May of 1940. The flight of Lea and Leo Moser from the nightmare of Nazi terror represents but a somber echo of the crises which faced untold millions in the spring of 1940. Were it not for the magnanimous intervention of one of the truly great women of our time, their story might have ended in an entirely different fashion.

With the German invasion of Holland, Leo resigned his position with Cristalleries de St.-Louis and fled with his daughter to Nice where they obtained South American passports. In June of 1940, Lea and Leo boarded the ship "Alsina" at the port of Marseille. As fate would have it, France fell to the Germans on June 21 and soon thereafter the Vichy government compelled the Alsina to put in at the port of Dakar in the French North African colony of Senegal. After a period of approximately six months, during which time the ship's passengers were forced to remain on board, the Alsina sailed for Morocco. Upon arrival in Casablanca the ship's entire complement was transferred to a concentration camp. With the capitulation of France, Leo's wife, Paolo, became justifiably concerned for the safety of her husband and daughter and appealed directly to Mrs. Eleanor Roosevelt for help. She was apparently quite successful. Based on a telegram issued on August 24, 1940, and undoubtedly initiated by Eleanor Roosevelt, temporary passports were authorized for Lea and Leo to enter the United States. In addition, Lea and Leo were mysteriously released from the Casablanca concentration camp and permitted to wend their way to Spain by any available conveyance. Traveling by way of Tangier and Seville, Lea and Leo arrived in Barcelona where they acquired U.S. passports. From Barcelona, the final leg of their journey took them to Lisbon, Portugal, where they boarded a Pan American Airlines plane for the United States. They arrived in New York in the spring of 1941.

From 1933 until the Nazi takeover of Czechoslovakia in 1938, the artistic glass output of the Moser works was primarily influenced by designs introduced prior to the departure of Leo Moser. Although the factory maintained a representation at international exhibitions, Brussels in 1935 and Paris in 1937, the worldwide market for artistic glass was in rapid decline. Under Nazi occupation, the board of directors was dissolved and all Moser stocks transferred to the control of the German government. Renamed the "Staatliche Glasmannfactur Karlsbad," the former Moser complex was converted to the production of items essential to the Nazi war effort. Many designers and artisans, who had previously been responsible for significant contributions to the field of artistic glass,

were interned as political prisoners in concentration camps. Those who remained worked virtually as slave labor—although, their labors were not entirely without reward. By deliberately altering melt ingredients and proportions, workers managed to produce tank windows and filter glasses which mysteriously cracked or shattered prior to their arrival at the front.

Early in 1945, on orders of the Nazis, the factory furnaces were extinguished. In May of that year, nine of the original factory workers joined to rebuild the ovens, and, on September 1, their efforts proved successful. Although the Moser works found itself in the Russian Zone at the end of World War II, an extensive reconstruction program, directed at regaining the works' former splendor, was systematically pursued. This program was highly successful, and the Moser works is now known under the name of the "Karlovaské Sklo" glassworks. Even though a significant portion of the artistic glass produced by the Karlovaské Sklo glassworks is based on the designs of important contemporary artists, its major output still relies heavily on glass designs executed prior to 1933. The continuing commercial success associated with these products is an undeniable tribute to the elegant and timeless beauty of the artistic glass realized under the directorship of the Moser family.

PARTIAL LISTING OF PARTICIPATION & AWARDS AT IMPORTANT EXHIBITIONS

1873—World Exhibition in Vienna (Medal for Workmanship)

1878—World Exhibition in Paris

1879—Industrial Fair in Teplice

1884—New Orleans

1889—Exhibition in Frankreich

1891—International Exhibition in Tasmania
—International Exhibition of Jamaica

1892—International Exhibition in Colombia
—Exhibition on the Isle of Man

1897—World Exhibition in Brussels

1900—World Exhibition in Paris (Silver Medal)

1902—1st International Exhibition of Modern
     Decorative Art in Turin
   —Austrian Art Exhibition in London

1904—World Exhibition in St. Louis

1905—World Exhibition in Liège

1906—German-Bohemian Exhibition
     (Recognition Diploma)
   —Exhibition of Applied Art in Liberec
     (Diploma for Workmanship)

1910—Exhibition in Belgium

1915—Pacific International Exposition in
     San Francisco (Medal of Award)

1921—International Exhibition in California

1925—International Exhibition of Decorative and
     Applied Art in Paris (Gold Medal—awarded
     outside the framework of competition)

1935—World Exhibition in Brussels

1937—World Exhibition in Paris

CHAPTER III, Selected References:
Fahdt, Julius, *Die Glasindustrie Oesterreich-Ungarns,* Dresden: Selbstverlag, 1901. "The 125th Anniversary of the Moser Glassworks at Karlovy Vary," *Czec. Glass Review,* Vol. 36 (1981) pp. 2-28. *Addressbuch Europas Glasindustrie,* Herausgegeben von der Redaktion der Seilschrift: "Die Glashütte," Dresden, 1925. Blau, Josef, *Die Glasmacher im Böhmer-und Bayerwald,* Regensburg: im Verlag Michael Lassleben Kallmunz, 1956. The Crystalex Branch Corporation, *Bohemian Glass,* Nový Bor, 1985. Villain, Jean, "The History of the Bohemian Glass Blowers," *Weltbuehne,* Ost Berlin, March 1960. "Leerdam Unica," 50 Jahre Modernes Niederlandisches Glas, Kunstmuseum Düsseldorf, 1977; Museum Boymans-van Beuningen Rotterdam, 1977. Bröhan, Sammlung Karl H., "Kunsthandwerk—Glas Holz Keramik," Berlin, 1976. Biographical information on Leo and Richard Moser was primarily obtained through personal interviews with members of the Moser family.

IV. MOSER ARTISTIC GLASS—CENTRAL EUROPEAN DESIGN INFLUENCES

According to an account given in *Czechoslovakian Glass,* the familiar allegation that Bohemian glass production was directly influenced by Italian immigrants in the 16th century cannot be supported by reliable evidence. There is little doubt, however, that Italian artistic concepts were copied and embellished by Bohemian artisans and that the importance of early Venetian glass in forming a backdrop for later Bohemian decorative styles cannot be overemphasized. During the latter half of the 16th century, much Venetian glassware was imported into Bohemia. This influx precipitated the adoption of enameling techniques and styles around 1570 which, although applied to Central European type forms, were Venetian in inspiration. Baroque decorative styles were introduced into Central Europe during the early 17th century and continued to dominate glass design until the emergence of Rococo forms around 1730. Within this time frame, Bohemian Baroque styles were strongly influenced by Italian as well as French glassmaking methods. After 1710, French adaptations of Baroque themes, which were to lay a foundation for the later Rococo, in addition to Bérain-inspired motifs,* were extensively employed by Bohemian glass engravers and decorators.

With the perfection of chalk glass in 1683, Bohemian designers were given access to an artistic medium capable of supporting innovative engraving at the highest design levels. Initial efforts at engraving this new crystal were uninspired; however, when deeper engraving techniques were applied around 1700, the quality of engraving improved rapidly. Symmetry and balanced proportions characterized Bohemian glass shapes during the first half of the 18th century. Panel faceting, a cutting technique designed to enhance visual appeal by taking advantage of the refractive properties of glass, was a dominant

feature of Bohemian Baroque glass during this period. It is interesting to note that much 19th- and 20th-century Bohemian glass, and, in particular, enameled glass marketed by the Moser firm, was manufactured with panels as an integral part of the mold-blown body. This attempt to emulate earlier facet-cut glass added an additional decorative dimension which significantly improved appearance without requiring costly cutting techniques.

A particularly noteworthy form of Bohemian Baroque glass was what is commonly referred to as "Zwischengoldglas" or "double-walled glass." Based on ancient decorative techniques of probable Jewish origin, Zwischengoldglas (literally, gold between glass), or its silver counterpart ("Zwichensilberglas"), was produced from the beginning of the 18th century and generally consisted of gold or silver foil, cut or etched to produce decorative patterns, sandwiched between two layers of glass for protection. Decorative motifs for Zwischengoldglas were strongly influenced by Italian Renaissance and Baroque styles. Examples of Zwischengoldglas, produced during the second half of the 19th century, are attributed to Ludwig Moser. Plate 3 illustrates a small beaker where the design has been worked in gold leaf using techniques essentially indistinguishable from those employed on later "Venetian" style glass; this unsigned example has been retained by the Moser family.

Although enameled glass was unfashionable during the first half of the 18th century, a particular form known as "Schwarzlot" ("black lead") enjoyed wide acceptance with wealthy clientele. In Bohemia, Schwarzlot is associated with the work of Daniel Preissler (1626-1733) and his son Ignaz (1676-1741) and was executed on clear glass using a shaded transparent black enamel. Inspired by engraved glass styles, Daniel Preissler is noted for his reliance on Baroque decorative elements while Ignaz Preissler is associated with grotesque and chinoiserie (Chinese-like) ornamentation. Schwarzlot is also characterized by the complementary application of gilding and

*Bérain, Jean, the Elder (1638-1711). Belgian-born painter, designer and engraver who was particularly skilled at adapting the works of earlier artists, in particular Raphael, to the contemporary Louis XIV style. Noted for his delicate arabesques and finely executed grotesques, Bérain's later work helped provide the basis of the Régence decorative form.

surface scratching to enliven details; on occasion, iron-red enameling was also employed. Toward the end of the 18th century, enameled decoration regained its lost popularity. During this period, however, enameling was mainly applied to souvenir items and often decorated by home decorators ("Hausmalers") operating at the heavily trafficked spa resorts. Although the decorative themes employed are not generally considered to be stylistically significant, they did provide a background for 19th-century decorators. Several elements in particular are relevant to "Venetian" style glass. For example, bright enamel colors were employed to decorate tableware with a variety of motifs including crests, stylized settings containing people surrounded by a Rococo cartouche, roses, garlands and floral bouquets.

Perhaps the single greatest influence on Bohemian Empire Period glass arose from the studio of Friedrich Egermann (1777-1864).* Egermann, whose artistic style featured detailed ornamentation as well as mythological and genre scenes, employed artists and artisans to create new glass types and decorative forms under his guidance. Predominantly known for the development of Lithyalin glass, the stylistic output of Egermann's studio, particularly with respect to the noted artist Alois Eiselt (Plate 1), apparently served as an inspiration to Moser enamelists working in the latter half of the 19th century (compare the decorative styles of the Moser vases in Plate 6 with that of Plate 1). Moser is known for the extensive use of insects as decorative highlights. This artistic form matured during the Empire period and was employed by the Egermann studio as well as by the Mistrovice engraver Florian Wander. Further influence was felt from France, where gilding and silvering of exquisite delicacy was applied to Opaline glass. Considered by many to be the finest work of its type ever performed, this latter art form consisted primarily of flowers, butterflies, insects and animals. The artist Jean-Francois Robert is best known for his association with this decorative style.

With the termination of the Napoleonic Wars and an upsurge in middle-class prosperity, the Bohemian Empire style of decoration was superceded by the Biedermeier period (c. 1825-1835). Of Germanic origin

*During the first quarter of the 19th century, Bohemian glassmakers adopted many French Empire decorative forms.

and principally applied to furniture styles, the Biedermeier form precipitated a distinctive alteration in Bohemian glass design. Bohemian manufacturers concentrated on the development of vividly colored glasses, such as Hyalith, Lithyalin and uranium-doped glasses, as well as engraved cased glass. Forms generally became massive with intricate facet cutting and engraving. Viennese Biedermeier style, for example, was typified by the work of Anton Kothgasser (1769-1851) and featured town and genre scenes, portraits and flowers; the use of lavish gilding was not uncommon.

After 1835, the resurgence of Second Rococo decorative styles in Europe partially displaced the production of Biedermeier glass in Bohemia. Rococo ornamentation, principally rocaille (rock-work), in conjunction with colors inspired by romantic painting were revived during this period. Prompted by French porcelain decorative themes, many glass items were enameled with female figures in romanticized period dress or with portraits of beautiful women. These artistic renditions were placed in a circular or oval setting and were often accented by intricate ornamental framing. Glassware reflecting this decorative style was produced by the Moser firm during the latter half of the 19th century. With the influx of the Second Rococo came the final ingredient for the development of two characteristic 19th-century Bohemian decorative forms. In addition to indigenous artistic styles, Italian Renaissance, as well as French Baroque and Rococo themes, became incorporated into an easily managed framework of artistic design. In order to differentiate these mature Bohemian styles from their parent fashions, the terms "Bohemian Renaissance" and "Bohemian Baroque" are often employed.

For about 30 years after the Biedermeier period, Bohemian glass exhibited little originality. When European and English styles changed to classical and neo-Renaissance forms in the 1860-1870's, most Bohemian manufacturers retained Biedermeier and Second Rococo decorative themes. Plate 6 illustrates several Moser enamel-decorated vases ostensibly manufactured between 1862 and 1870. These vases represent some of the earliest documented Moser examples and strongly reflect the Bohemian glass manufacturing philosophy prevalent during this time. Under pressure from foreign competition and in the face of increased demand for Bohemian products abroad, the quality of manufactured glassware declined during the 1860-1870 period. Cased glass, employed for multicolor engraving during the Biedermeier, was superseded by less costly stained glass. Engraving techniques became commercialized, with a subsequent reduction in overall quality. Much of the poorly engraved stained glass recognized by most Americans as "Bohemian" originated within this time frame.

During the 1870-1880 period, glass decorated by the Moser firm was beginning to exhibit the unique properties by which Moser enameled glass can be recognized. Prior to this time, little definitive information exists regarding the decorative styles employed by Moser enamelists. It is probably reasonable, however, to assume that in many instances engraved and enameled decorative styles ran parallel to one another. From the founding of the company in 1857, designers and engravers employed by Moser relied heavily on past artistic styles: for instance, from Rococo masters such as A. Watteau, Boucher and J. H. Fragonard. With the hiring of top-quality engravers, Moser engraving became characterized by precise and detailed execution of figural compositions, ornaments, small emblems and initials; these properties are also quite evident in the enameled glass produced by Moser. Plate 4 illustrates an unsigned lidded container dating from the 1840 to 1880 period. The glass body of this example, heavily doped with uranium, is executed in the Biedermeier style with an eight-point mitre-cut star on the base. Seven of the eight face-cut sides have a raised circular panel (cabochon) enameled with fruit or insects surrounded by a Rococo cartouche. Multicolored stained panels with engraved decoration were also characteristic of the Biedermeier style. The pitcher and covered box in Plate 5 are early examples exhibiting profuse floral enameling applied to stained panels of varying colors. Although, in the absence of signatures, it may seem presumptuous to attribute these examples to Moser decorators, the extensive use of gold and enamel in intricate and restless designs bears a strong resemblance to later documented Moser works.

By 1870 a series of artistic revivals, inspired partially by nationalistic themes and partially by the formation of museum collections of antique glassware, began to influence Bohemian glass styles. Initial response to these revivals was the reintroduction of glassware and enameled decorations executed in 16th- and 17th-century styles. This German and Bohemian neo-Renaissance glass remained popular from 1870 to 1890. Islamic style glass decoration was introduced by J.&L. Lobmeyr, Meyr's Neffe and Ludwig Moser during the 1870's (Plates 31, 32 and 33). In 1878, Moser exhibited heavily gilded glass decorated with Japanese inspired motifs (Plate 54). J.&L. Lobmeyr first displayed iridescent glass in 1873 and commercial production began at Neuwelt in Bohemia. Iridescent glass was exhibited by a large number of Bohemian factories at the 1878 Paris Exhibition. By 1879, a large selection of Bohemian iridescent and bronze glass was being exported to the United States. Although comparatively rare, iridescent glass, generally decorated using enamel-gilding techniques, was marketed by Moser (Plates 33 and 67). In the 1890's, Bohemia produced large quantities of enameled glass decorated to resemble English cameo styles. By applying heavy enamel to acid-etched colored grounds, facsimiles were produced bearing a close resemblance to the prototype. Marketed under the names of "Florentine Art Cameo" and "Lace de Bohème Cameo," these imitations successfully destroyed the demand for the more expensive cameo glass. Although Moser produced some early cameo glass, to the authors' knowledge no enameled facsimiles were produced by that factory. "Mary Gregory" style glass was produced extensively in Europe and examples of this glass type are known to have been marketed by Moser.

World markets had attained a sufficiently high level of competitiveness by the 1880's that the more advanced manufacturing techniques practiced in England and the United States were largely adopted by Bohemian glasshouses. These technologies paved the way for the innovative Art Nouveau styles which later rose to international prominence. The Art Nouveau movement (called "Jugendstil" in Germany and "Secession" in Austria) was firmly entrenched in Bohemia by 1895. By far, the most extensively produced Bohemian product in this category was iridescent colored glass executed with techniques introduced by Louis Comfort Tiffany. Although initially produced and exhibited by Johann Löetz Witwe, iridescent art glass of this type was also manufactured by such noted factories as the Králik glassworks in Lenora, Harrach in Neuwelt, by both glassworks in Kôstany, and in the Pallme-König and Rundskoff factories. Colored iridescent glass of the typical "Loetz" type which can be attributed to Ludwig Moser is unknown to the authors. Koloman Moser, however, independently executed designs for E. Bakalowitz Söhn which were subsequently produced by Löetz, Meyr's Neffe and the Rheinische Glashütten.

Engraved Art Nouveau glass was also popular throughout Bohemia. Based on floral themes, this form of engraving was generally executed on clear crystal. Perhaps the most famous product of the Moser factory was deep engraved Art Nouveau glass produced by using shaded blanks of high purity crystal. After approximately 1900, a rift in artistic ideas occurred at the Moser factory which led to the introduction of a new Art Nouveau form. This new style, known as "Karlsbader Secession Glass," was not particularly popular and was apparently produced for only a short time period (Plate 120).

Although the Art Nouveau influence in Central Europe was actually on the decline by 1905, the outbreak of World War I erased all remaining vestiges of this artistic form. After 1918, new art forms, partially based on concepts formalized prior to the war and partially dependent on individual artists and design groups, were introduced. Shortly after 1900, a "Modern" school of design was founded, with a Prague professor of architecture, Jan Kotêra, as its most influential proponent. Based on Baroque cut-glass styles, Modern glass design stressed the architectural quality of glass shapes, their function and the optical properties of the base metal. A spin-off of this movement, the Artel group of artists, introduced Cubism to furniture and ceramic design and, through the efforts of the architect Josef Rosipal, to glass forms. This latter group, although initially of little influence, formed the basis of the Bohemian Art Deco style which emerged after 1925. Moser interpreted the concepts of Kotêra (Figure 9) by producing a

new line of glassware which we will refer to as the "Modern" style. This form of glass decoration, which emphasized facet-cutting techniques designed to enhance and accentuate the jewel-like properties of the base metal, was produced in various forms by Moser well into the 1930's. Rare-earth doped glasses, introduced after 1920, proved to be a perfect medium for the execution of Modern and Art Deco designs. Articles produced using these unique glasses brought the Moser firm well deserved recognition.

As artistic director of the Moser firm, Leo Moser exhibited a high level of artistic and technical expertise. From a constant study of glass chemistry emerged the commercial practicality of rare-earth doped glasses, as well as an extensive palette of subtle glass colors eminently suited to the crystal-cutting styles which characterized Moser production. In a more practical vein, Leo collaborated with scientists at the Kaiser Wilhelm Institute in Berlin to develop an unbreakable clear glass which was marketed under the name "Dural." Always interested in techniques which could simultaneously cut production costs yet retain overall quality, Leo participated in the development of polishing and cutting machines, as well as manual procedures, which could rapidly perform precise, repetitive operations. Molded glass, which heretofore had been produced in limited quantities, was introduced to a broader spectrum of artistic glass products. When the effects of world-wide depression produced a marketing crisis which threatened to precipitate a financial collapse of the Moser firm, Leo drew heavily on these innovative developments to stem the tide of bankruptcy. Unfortunately, a predictable shift in social emphasis toward functionalism and low cost destroyed a major portion of the luxury glass market, and the Moser firm remained at a bare subsistence level until the Nazi takeover in 1938.

CHAPTER IV, Selected References:
Pešatová, Zuzana, *Bohemian Engraved Glass,* Prague: Knihtisk, 1968. Schmidt, Robert, *Lobmeyer, 1823-1923.* Wein: Anton Schroll & Co. The Corning Museum of Glass, *Czechoslovakian Glass,* New York: Dover Publications, 1981. Drahotova, Olga, *European Art Glass,* New York: Excalibur Books, 1983. *The Smithsonian Illustrated Library of Antiques.* "Glass," prepared by the Cooper-Hewitt Museum, 1979. Definitions of decorative styles referred to in this chapter can be obtained from Newman, Harold, *An Illustrated Dictionary of Glass,* London: Thames and Hudson Ltd., 1977.

V. DECORATIVE STYLES BY CATEGORY

In order to facilitate the identification of individual examples and their associated time periods, the authors have chosen to partition Moser glass into generic categories based on prominent decorative features and/or techniques. Throughout its history, the Moser firm was not a noted producer of classical Art Glass which relies exclusively on free-blown form and color for its artistic merit. Although individual artists, such as Chris Lebeau, influenced the limited production of Art Glass forms, the vast majority of items marketed by Moser must be listed under the general heading of decorated or artistic glass. Characterized by the extensive use of engraving, cutting and/or enameling, Moser artistic glass can be classified under the following major headings:

CUT AND ENGRAVED GLASS
  * Engraved Glass
  * Art Nouveau
  * Cameo
  * Cut Glass
  * Rare-Earth Doped Glasses
  * Weiner Werkstätte/Art Deco

ENAMELED GLASS
  * Enamel-gilt Decoration
  * German neo-Renaissance Glass
  * High Relief Decoration
  * Acanthus Ornamentation
  * Aquatic Life Forms
  * Venetian Style Glassware
  * Large Floral Enameling
  * Ungilded Enamel on Glass

MOLDED GLASS

A. CUT AND ENGRAVED GLASS

Engraved Glass

Engraving on glass was the artistic foundation upon which the Moser firm built its international reputation for excellence. Of all the techniques available to the glass decorator, engraving is the most difficult and time consuming; consummate skill is required in the creation of even the most seemingly insignificant monograms. Although Moser engraving is typically characterized by detailed and precise execution, it must be remembered that there was a considerable variation in skill even among Moser engravers. That variation, when coupled to a market ranging from relatively inexpensive spa souvenirs to singular artistic masterpieces designated for the crowned heads of Europe, resulted in a rather broad spectrum of engraving techniques and finished quality.

Ludwig Moser built a personal reputation upon his expert engraving of hunting and woodland scenes, ornaments, monograms, writings and seals. Although these themes remained a staple of the Moser firm through the latter half of the 19th century, they were complemented by the addition of floral and Baroque themes of exquisite beauty, as well as finely detailed figural motifs based on the works of 18th-century romantic masters. After 1890, Moser engraving became increasingly influenced by the Art Nouveau movement. This style continued to dominate Moser production up to approximately 1905, after which the artistic emphasis shifted away from engraving toward glass-cutting techniques which stressed the jewel-like properties of the crystal mass. Throughout the 1920's and 1930's, Moser retained an excellent reputation for high quality engraving; however, this expertise was primarily applied to the ornamentation of customized table services and never again achieved the commercial level of importance it enjoyed during the 19th century.

Engraved Moser glass, appearing comparatively infrequently on the American market, is generally difficult to identify unless associated with glass styles which, by themselves, are unquestionably related to Moser. Certainly one of the most common forms encountered is illustrated in Plate 11. These examples combine precision cutting with gold-filled engraving on distinctively colored five-layer cased, clear-to-emerald-green blanks. We estimate that engraved glass of this type was manufactured toward the end of the 19th century. Based on an original model in the Prague Museum, the goblet in Plate 167 is engraved with a classical Bohemian woodland scene. Engraved and graduated cups, from which spa visitors could partake of the healing waters, remained a stable commercial enterprise throughout the years of the firm's existence. Plates 7 and 8 include three engraved spa cups of traditional design.

Art Nouveau

Art Nouveau became popular in Central Europe around 1895 and dominated artistic styles for a decade. As a general rule, Bohemian engraved Art Nouveau forms emphasized floral motifs executed on clear crystal blanks; shaded glass was rarely employed. The mainstream of Moser Art Nouveau glass, on the other hand, is characterized by the application of engraving techniques, developed initially by seal and gem cutters, to the generation of deeply engraved floral forms on heavy, high quality, shaded glass blanks; although comparatively rare, clear crystal was also employed. Engraved decoration consisted of undulating asymmetrical compositions of stems, leaves and flowers, sometimes complemented by the addition of enamel and gold; wild roses, day lilies and irises were favorite artistic subjects. Drinking goblets in supple Art Nouveau forms resembling the calixes (cup or chalice) of flowers were also produced (Plates 116 and 118). In its most common form, Moser Art Nouveau deep-engraved glass exhibits a gradual shading from a clear base to a colored top. Many glasses of this type were constructed from five-cased layers with the heavy outer layer of clear crystal, on which the deeply engraved motifs were worked, constituting at least 90% of the total glass thickness (refer to Chapter VI; glass fabrication). A thin intermediate layer of colored glass of variable thickness provided the shading. Glass colors developed by Moser soon after the opening of the Meierhöfen works, which included deep shades of ruby, cobalt blue, emerald green and amethyst mauve, were primarily employed for Art Nouveau glass forms. Engraved Art Nouveau glass similar to that produced by Moser was also marketed by Graf Harrach in Neuwelt and Feix's in Albrechtice.

Occasionally, Moser Art Nouveau designs were embellished by the application of heavy glass insets (sometimes referred to as "padding" or "marquetry"). These insets were generally floral forms with carefully controlled outlines to accurately portray the element desired. They were fused to the background metal when at the working temperature and were cameo cut, in contrast to the deep intaglio cutting employed on the remainder of the piece (Plates 117, 118 and 119).

Around 1900, Moser introduced a new type of glassware characterized by the combination of red and green or violet glass insets, matt green enameling, heavy high-relief, gold-enamel stems and intaglio-cut insects and birds (Plate 120). Produced under the name "Karlsbader Secession," this new glass style retained the Art Nouveau essence but represented a definite break from the deeply engraved Art Nouveau crystal produced prior to this time. Karlsbader Secession type glass was manufactured in tableware as well as purely decorative items, and it is recorded that quantities were purchased for use by the royal family at Castle Ehrenfeld. A lack of popularity compared to that of deeply engraved Art Nouveau crystal, and occasional color bleeding encountered during the manufacturing process, limited the production of Karlsbader Secession glass.

Cameo

Beginning with John Northwood's copy of the Portland Vase, completed in 1876, there was a steady increase in the popularity of cameo glass. It was not until the 1880's, however, that the advent of acid/wheel cutting (acid rough cutting combined with a wheel-cut final finish) and acid cut-back techniques increased the availability of cameo glass to the general public. Following the English lead, Bohemian factories flooded the European and American markets with bi-level cameo designs produced rapidly with the aid of hydroflouric acid. In the area of cameo production, Moser's greatest output consisted of articles having friezes (bands) of acid cut-back decoration. Although subject matter and cutting styles changed over the years, this particular decorative format persisted until well after World War I. Early frieze decoration was generally executed in a wide band, using a single acid cutting and with only the raised surfaces being gilded; a popular theme consisted of elephants and palm trees in a single setting (Plate 131). Examples embellished with additional gold-enamel decoration or cut from cased glass have been recorded. Later work of this type, introduced just prior to World War I, was typically applied to Modern style glass, was scaled down in width compared to earlier examples, and had the frieze area totally gilded with matt burnished raised areas; Amazon warriors were a widely used decorative motif during this period (Plates 137 and 138). Around 1900 Moser produced limited quantities of acid/wheel cut cameo of exceptional quality. Acid-cut cased cameo in the style of late Gallé and ungilded, acid cut-back cameo on single color glass was also produced by Moser.

Acid cut-back cameo techniques were applied to tableware as well as purely decorative items. Gilded acid cut-back borders, bands and accents, similar to those employed by the Honesdale Decorating Co., were common (Plates 145, 150 and 194). Plate 182 illustrates tableware fully cut in a cameo Rococo motif which features gilded highlighting with a stippled acid-cut surround; this form, which incorporates Moser lead crystal in its design, post-dates World War I.

Cut Glass

With the development of chalk glass around 1685, a medium of high clarity became available to Bohemian engravers and cutters. In addition to a rock-crystal-like appearance, its inherent hardness permitted the use of decorative techniques heretofore reserved for stone cutting. Bohemian cut glass of this formative period was characterized by panel faceting combined with oval facets designed to enhance the elegance and brilliance of a particular design. Quite often, cutting was combined with engraving or enameling to achieve striking decorative effects. Prior to 1900, Moser employed cutting primarily as an adjunct to engraving or enameling. Early Moser styles were predominantly based on Biedermeier and Baroque themes which combined panel faceting, flute cutting and the use of raised oval panels, referred to as "cabochons" (Plates 2, 3 and 4), with intricate engraved or enameled decoration. During the Art Nouveau period, glass

cutting gradually rose to new levels of importance, until, with the introduction of an extensive palette of colored crystal after World War I, cutting fully dominated Moser artistic styles.

Shortly after 1900 a new concept in glass design was developed in Bohemia. Jan Kotêra, a professor of architecture at the Academy of Applied Arts in Prague, was the primary protagonist of this movement which was principally based on early Baroque cut glass styles. Kotêra stressed the architectural characterisics of glass shapes, their functional properties and the optical quality of the metal. These principles were adopted by the Moser firm for the production of a new line of flawless, heavy cut crystal which emphasized the jewel-like properties of the glass medium. By concentrating on refractive and reflective effects created by carefully controlling glass thickness in conjunction with exacting face-cutting techniques, a style of sufficient universal appeal was developed whose popularity remains undiminished to the present day. The majority of articles produced in this so-called "Modern" style are characterized by a series of contiguous facet-cut vertical panels which follow the design contours of the piece. Plate 174 illustrates a beaker which typifies this decorative style. A Moser developed spin-off of the Kotêra style featured wide, delicately outlined panels which were typically concave in form (Plate 202).* These latter designs provided the basis for what Leo Moser would later refer to as "commercial art glass." Moser rarely, if ever, produced cut glass in the style which was popular during the American "Brilliant" period (c. 1876-1915), although elements of that form were sometimes employed to enhance, rather than dominate, a particular decorative motif. In combination with Art Deco and Wiener Werkstätte designs, which were primarily produced after 1920, the "Modern" style of cutting remained commercially popular well into the 1930's.

A vast majority of Moser cut glass was marketed as tableware and it was through this artistic form, perhaps more than any other, that Moser glass achieved international recognition. Geometrically precise cutting, high purity crystal, delicately balanced design and intricately engraved or enameled mono-

*As recorded in *Kunsthandwerk-Glas Holz Keramik* (Sammlung Karl H. Brohan, Berlin, 1976), many of these designs can be attributed to the artists Bayerl, Bohn, Ortlieb and Schoder.

gramming were Moser trademarks; these characteristics are clearly evident in the "Royal" pattern wine service illustrated in Plate 151. Cut glass, not designated for table use, falls collectively under the Moser designated classification of "Fantazie" Moser.

Rare-Earth Doped Glasses

Experiments performed by the German chemist Auer concerning the effects of introducing rare-earth oxides into a glass melt, in conjunction with the commercial availability of rare-earth oxides after 1920, led to the production of new and distinctive glass types by the Moser firm. These glasses were first produced in quantity by Moser and probably represent the culmination of a joint research effort by Leo Moser, Professor Quasebart of the Auer-Gesellschaft in Berlin, and Professor Turner of the English Glass Research Institute, Sheffield. Rare-earth oxides are relatively weak colorants; consequently, high concentrations are required to produce a reasonably dense shading. This fact, in combination with high material cost, limited the use of rare-earth oxides to fairly expensive artware.

As registered in the factory melt journals, Moser produced a multiplicity of rare-earth glasses. Those which actually appear to have been marketed are listed in Table I. Many of these glasses are identified in Moser-related literature for the first time and the colors associated with several of them remain unknown to the authors at the time of this printing. Alexandrit, by far the most common rare-earth glass, contains 4 to 5% neodymium oxide by weight and appears a pale bluish-violet under fluorescent illumination and red-violet in natural sunlight or under tungsten illumination. Royalit, a very costly glass to manufacture, was produced by combining neodymium oxide with selenium. Each of the rare-earth glasses exhibits the property of changing apparent color, depending on thickness and background illumination. This characteristic was exploited by employing special glass-cutting techniques to visually enhance specific designs. Success in design was witnessed by the Moser firm's being awarded a gold medal at the International Exhibition of Decorative Arts in Paris in 1925. (This award was particularly prestigious since it was presented outside the framework of the established competition.) While rare-earth doped glasses are generally found in the Modern or Art Deco styles (with occasional decorative engraving), simpler hand-formed variations based on older styles, such as the cologne bottle in Plate 165, can be found.

As a point of interest, the cologne bottle in Plate 165 is signed with an acid-etched Moser signature and bears a Meyr's Neffe paper label (Figure 23). It is

TABLE I: RARE-EARTH GLASSES

Designation	Rare Earth	Color
Alexandrit	Neodymium (Nd)	blue-violet to red-violet (Plate 166)
Alexandritbleiglas (lead glass)	Nd	blue-violet to red-violet
Didym (Ditit)	Nd, Praseodymium (Pr)	blue-gray
Heliolit (I)	Nd, Pr, Lanthanum (La)	unknown
Heliolit (II)	Nd, Pr	pinkish-brown
Heliolit W/119	Nd, Pr	pinkish-brown (Plate 178)
Latr W/89	Nd, Pr	pinkish-brown
Latr W/120	Nd, Pr	unknown
Latr 2/8.28	Nd, Pr	unknown
Latr P/1	Pr	unknown
Latr P/2	Pr	unknown
Latr P/3	La	unknown
Latr P/4	Pr	unknown
Praseamit	Pr	greenish-yellow
Royalit	Nd	brownish-red (Plate 163)

probable that the lighter-weight, free-formed Alexandrit examples were made at the Adolf works, while the heavier crystal blanks destined for the cutting shop were manufactured at Meierhöfen.

Weiner Werkstätte/Art Deco

Much of the Weiner Werkstätte's success can be attributed to the creative talents of its co-founder, Josef Hoffman. A professor at the Vienna School of Arts and crafts, the founder of the Wiener Werkbundes in 1912, an exhibitor at the Austrian Museum Exhibition in Vienna from 1911 to 1914, and a recognized leader in the design of silver, art glass and tableware, Hoffman exerted a dominant influence over most artists with whom he came in contact. Silver designs by Koloman Moser, Dagobert Peche (1887-1923) and Josef Hoffman are considered the quintessence of Art Deco form. Hoffman's Art Deco designs, in particular, are noted for their distinguished and dignified character. Many glass designs executed by Josef Hoffman prior to World War I were subsequently produced by Moser. These works primarily served as the decorative elements for goblets, lamp shades, bookends and ornaments and consisted of facet cutting, as well as molded forms of animals, nude women and foliate decorations in opaque black and purple glass. Designs by Hoffman are usually signed "J. Hoffman" in engraved script on the base.

Over the years there were many Wiener Werkstätte designers involved with the production of artistic glass. Of these, only the names of a few of the most prominent will be mentioned. Machael Powalny (1871-1954) was co-founder with Berthold Löffer of the Wiener Keramik (ceramics), professor at the Vienna School of Arts and Crafts from 1909 to 1941 and a noted designer of Art Deco porcelain figures as early as 1914. Powalny preferred to work on a matt-finish glass surface which he decorated with primitive patterns and signs of the zodiac. Dagobert Peche was a member of the Wiener Werkstätte from 1915 to 1923 and the director of its Zurich branch in 1917-1918. Peche specialized in simple floral motifs and, as mentioned previously, was considered one of the foremost designers of Art Deco silver. Otto Prutscher (1880-1949) was a student of Josef Hoffman and a professor at the Vienna School of Arts and Crafts.

Prutscher designed cut, patterned and iridescent glass and was an important Viennese silversmith in the 1920's. Vally Wieselthier (1895-1945) became famous for his porcelain figurines produced by the Rosenthal factory. Additional artists and designers of note include Hilda Jesser (born 1894), Reni Schaschl, Mathilde Flögl, Leopold Bauer, Eduard Josef Wimmer (1882-1961), Julius Zimpel (1896-1925) and Fritzi Löw-Lazar (born 1892).

Most of the Wiener Werkstätte designs produced by Moser can be recognized by their characteristic shallow "S" shaped bowls; this form is typified by the wedding cup in Plate 183. Light-weight, free-formed examples (Plate 183), or heavier Modern style cut forms (Plate 181) can be found. A specific series of dark, richly shaded glasses was designated for Wiener Werkstätte use in the factory melt journal.

B. ENAMELED GLASS

Enamel-gilt Decoration

Gilding and enameling have often been combined to create decorative design elements. One technique used extensively in Europe and the United States was to outline the design element with gold, fix the gold in a muffle kiln, and then complete the design by filling in the element with enamel; a second firing fused the enamel to the ground. This technique is readily identified by the existence of well-defined boundaries between the gilding and enamel. A second decorative technique was to first lay down enamel to emphasize a design in relief, fire the enamel in a kiln, and then overcoat the enamel and define the boundaries of the design element with gilding which was fired to fix the entire design. Characteristically, this second technique completely overcoated the enamel; it is only through observation of the pattern from the reverse side that the existence of an enameled layer becomes obvious. A third technique was to lay down a combination of opaque enamel and gold (or silver) and to fire them simultaneously in a kiln. As a result, gold and enamel mixed during the firing process, eliminating any well-defined boundary between the two mediums. This latter technique, which we refer to as "composite gold-enameling," was extensively employed by Moser decorators, but all three variants can be found on Moser glass.

Composite gold-enameling appears to have been accomplished by applying an opaque enamel to the ground to be decorated and then fully or partially overcoating the enamel with gold. During firing, the enamel would displace the gold at the high points of the design; the relative visibility of the enamel would depend on the distribution and thickness of the gold overcoat. For finely detailed elements, such as twigs or outlines, it appears at first glance that the enamel was initially applied over a gold background. This, however, was not the case. Protrusion of enamel through the gold is a critical factor in identifying this decorative technique, and, at times, careful observation is required to recognize this characteristic. Distinguishing between gold and enamel is made more difficult since yellow and orange enamels were generally employed. Other colors, such as lavender and aqua, were used with gold, but such combinations are comparatively rare.

Pure gold applied to untreated glass is easily removed by abrasive action. Moser extensively employed high-lustre gold for such decorative highlights as rim and body banding and interstitial patterns. Matt gold (or silver) surfaces could be created by applying gold leaf or powder mixed with a fixative, such as honey, to the ground. After firing, the metal would exhibit a matt finish which could be burnished to a high lustre if desired. Moser decorators applied gold finishes to untreated glass, acid-etched glass and glass which was first coated with a thin layer of transparent enamel. Matt and high-lustre finishes were employed in similar capacities; however, matt gold and silver were particularly used as pattern fillers, i.e., for the interior of leaves or flowers which were outlined in composite gold-enamel. The higher durability of these matt finishes, probably due to their greater initial thickness, made them an ideal ground for further decoration, and they were employed in that capacity more frequently than their high-lustre counterparts. When gold was employed as a ground, it was fixed in a kiln prior to the application of additional decorative elements. As a result, the glass visually exhibits a uniform coating when viewed from the reverse side. Composite gold-enamel was apparently applied to a metal ground by using the same techniques employed for its direct application on glass.

Transparent enamels were occasionally used in conjunction with composite gold-enamel to achieve striking decorative effects (Plate 41). Elements formed by transparent enamels were generally outlined and highlighted in gold.

Reliable authorities agree that the quality of enameled decoration in Bohemia was in a state of decline by the turn of the 20th century. Due in part to an increased awareness of glass per se as a unique art form, competitive pressures to produce glassware in ever-increasing quantities compelled factory managers to search for decorative techniques amenable to mass production. Moser was not immune to this metamorphosis which produced a recognizable alteration in decorative styles. Prior to the opening of the Meierhöfen works in 1893, Moser enameled glass was characterized by the production of ornate and intricate floral and Rococo themes which fully covered the glass blanks to which they were applied. In many cases, decorative forms reflected prevailing artistic styles indigenous to the North Bohemian area surrounding Meistersdorf. Typified by the examples in Plates 14, 39, 46 and 63, enameled glassware produced during this period is highly sought after by contemporary collectors.

From about 1895 to the start of World War I, enamel-gilt decorative patterns, while retaining the essence of previous floral and Rococo designs, became abbreviated in form. Rather than forming a totally dominate artistic expression, enameling began to complement the glass forms to which it was applied (Plates 124, 127 and 133). With the conclusion of World War I and the relative economic stability provided by the Bohemian Union Bank, a definite refinement in enameling techniques became evident. While still retaining earlier artistic elements, decorative patterns became light and fresh in appearance, and there was a noticeable improvement in technical execution (Plates 156, 159, 189, 192). Much of this change was undoubtedly related to the purchase of Meyr's Neffe Adolf glassworks in 1922. Consideration of the decorative patterns, quality of execution and refinements in glass processing leads to the conclusion that enamel-gilt decorated glass marketed by Moser during the 1920's and 1930's equals or surpasses that produced during the 19th century.

German Neo-Renaissance Glass

After 1870, newly organized glassmaking schools, i.e., Steinschönau in 1857 and Haida in 1870, both located in northern Bohemia, advocated the return to earlier glass styles. This movement occurred when Bismarck and the Prussian monarchy were engaged in the struggle for German unification and served to highlight the common historical bond which existed between the various German states. Glass forms primarily copied 16th- and early 17th-century Central European Renaissance styles and were decorated with enameled patterns derived from 15th- and 16th-century Italian decorative arts. Glass was typically green, yellow-green and, sometimes, clear in color and was decorated with prunts, multicolored enamel beading, coats of arms, kings, knights, hunters and hunting emblems. It was not uncommon for the glass forms to be scaled-down versions of the originals or even to assume contemporary shapes for functional purposes.

Full neo-Renaissance glassware was primarily manufactured between 1870 and 1890. Harrach of Neuwelt, Meyr's Neffe in Winterberg and the studio of Ambrose Egermann (eldest son of Frederich Egermann) were among the most noted producers of this glass type. Plate 51 illustrates a pair of pedestal salts decorated in the German neo-Renaissance style; they are unsigned, but, from known provenance, were purchased from the Moser factory in 1880. As is characteristic of the vast majority of German neo-Renaissance glass, signed examples of Moser's work in this decorative style are unknown to the authors.

High-Relief Decoration

High-relief decoration of a glass body can be obtained by applying heavy or multiple layers of enamel, fused beading, lamp/oven-work or precast glass forms to the surface, or by attaching decorative elements with a low-temperature adhesive. Decoration of this type is recognized as being characteristic of the North Bohemian glassmaking centers surrounding Haida and Steinschönau. Each of the above techniques was apparently employed by Moser decorators during the firm's tenure at Meistersdorf; however, the use of preformed acorns and bees has become accepted as a unique Moser trademark. Although details are un-known, cast decorations were most likely produced by melting glass beads or powder (pâte de verre) in a ceramic mold prepared using the lost-wax process. Larger cast items were fused directly to the glass substrate prior to the application of decorative enamel. Smaller elements, particularly those used in quantity, were enameled or gilded prior to application. Cast objects are found in many varying forms which include birds, acorns, flowers, fish and aquatic forms, faceted jewels, insects, reptiles, leaves and grape clusters. Many of the more lavishly decorated items are found with precast elements in combination with lamp/ovenwork forms such as rigaree, stems, leaves, fruits and flowers. Glass beading was also employed to form grape clusters, provide jeweled highlights and form multicolor coralene decoration.

Plates 81, 82 and 83 illustrate an enameling technique employed by Moser decorators to create delicate floral forms in high relief. Petals and complete flowers were individually formed and shaded prior to firing in a kiln. Several North Bohemian firms produced similar high quality floral work. Fortunately, decorative styles were sufficiently different and specific manufacturers' products can generally be isolated. A rather coarse rendition of this decorative technique, originating from Nový Bor in Bohemia, as well as Italy after World War II, is readily available to the glass collector. There should be no difficulty, however, in differentiating between the exquisitely executed early examples illustrated in this book and the much later highly commercialized versions.

As a possible aid in dating and identifying Moser glass, we wish to note that glass acorns (Plate 80), insects (Plate 61), flowers (Plate 32), etc., were generally attached to the glass ground with an opaque cream-colored enamel. These decorative elements were enameled only on their exposed sides. In contrast, applied bees were not formed from glass, but rather were constructed using a lightweight plastic interior completely covered with a heavy gold-colored metal foil. Bees were attached to the base glass by means of a transparent low-temperature adhesive and are consequently more easily removed than their enamel-fused counterparts. Based on the majority of decorative styles which incorporate cast decorative elements or preformed bees, we have concluded that cast elements were primarily employed prior to 1890 while the use of preformed bees came after that date.

Acanthus Ornamentation

A common thread linking all items decorated in the Acanthus Ornamentation style is acanthus scroll-work executed in brilliant enameled colors. In some instances this leaf-like decorative motif is combined with a repetitive series of half ovals defined by a matt-gold ground rimmed with white enamel and having centered enameled dots of varying color. Known as "Fish Scale," this latter decorative element can be found on 16th- and 17th-century Italian glass. Plate 30 illustrates a wine decanter having a decorative pattern which combines the elements of acanthus scroll and fish-scale ornamentation. This decanter was commissioned by J.&L. Lobmeyr (table set no. 81) during the 1880-1890 period and was produced at Meyr's Neffe's Adolf works. A similarly decorated footed goblet is attributed to Meyr's Neffe in *Českísklo—XIX Stoleti* (Plate 261). Page 261 of *Historisimus* by Barbara Mundt illustrates a beaker and pitcher marketed by J.&L. Lobmeyr in 1873 which is heavily decorated with fish-scale ornamentation in the style of the water set in Plate 28. Examples of this latter type probably also originated from Meyr's Neffe.

Acanthus Ornamentation was apparently a rather popular decorative theme since, in addition to Meyr's Neffe, it was produced by Moser, Graf Harrach, the Riedel Glassworks and S. Reich & Co. Plate 35 illustrates a mounted vase combining Acanthus Ornamentation with a typical Moser decorative pattern. This vase, and the decanter in Plate 36, are probably stylistically representative of the 19th-century Acanthus Ornamentation produced by Moser. As evidenced by the examples in Plate 159, Moser continued to employ Acanthus Ornamentation well into the 20th century. Although variations of Acanthus Ornamentation were produced by several companies, examples which conform both in design and details of execution to those illustrated in this book probably share a common origin.

Aquatic Lifeforms

Aquatic lifeforms were a favorite theme of Moser decorators. Although stylized aquatic forms occur rather frequently in French glass of the late 19th and early 20th centuries and from ancient times have been incorporated as design elements in glass manufactured throughout the world, as an aggregate, this type of decoration is relatively rare. Considering the commonality of glass types, shapes and decorative themes, glass decorated with aquatic forms was apparently produced by Moser in rather large quantities. It seems doubtful that any other glass company set out to create as extensive a product line based solely on aquatic decorative motifs. In general, such items produced by Moser can be recognized by the anatomical accuracy of the enameling and/or applied forms in combination with a glass color, texture and form which enhances the visual effect of an aquatic environment (Plates 17, 62, 106 and 128). Later highly stylized versions were also produced; the example in Plate 144 shows a distinct departure from the earlier more naturalistic forms.

Venetian Style Glassware

Origins of the Venetian style glassware presented in this book remain controversial; however, rather than dismissing the subject in an offhand manner, we will endeavor to acquaint the reader with some established credentials of this interesting glass type. Common to the mainstream of Venetian style glassware is the use of a decorative motif composed of a gilded Baroque cartouche, surrounding portraits or personages in 18th-century dress, combined with bouquets and garlands of enameled roses (Plate 196). In addition to this rather distinctive decoration, the glass employed was generally of a vibrant ruby-red, green or cobalt-blue color and emulated early Venetian refining and fabrication techniques. Venetian style glass is typically fragile, of excellent quality and light in weight. Footed items such as compotes, goblets, etc., generally have folded-under rim bases; plates and bowls have applied circular cross-section base rims; and where pontil marks occurred they were normally left unfinished.

From a historical design standpoint, the decorative themes on Venetian style glassware are characteristically Bohemian. Zwischengoldglas is an ancient decorative technique consisting of gold foil, scribed or cut by a sharp instrument to produce decorative patterns, sandwiched between two protective layers of glass (Plate 3). Plate 26 in *Czechoslovakian Glass* illustrates a Bohemian Zwischengoldglas plate, dating from the 1698-1710 time frame, which bears a striking resemblance to the hand-scribed gilded Baroque decoration present on Venetian style glassware. It is also interesting to observe that late 18th-century Bohemian enameled tableware consisted predominately of crests or stylized landscapes containing personages in period dress surrounded by frames of Rococo ornaments. During this same period, clear or opaque white glass decorated with motifs of roses, garlands and bouquets of flowers was quite popular.

Proper attribution of Venetian style glassware is somewhat confusing. Although the decorative motifs appear to be of Bohemian origin, the base glass to which the decoration is applied most likely originated at Murano. This conclusion is not only substantiated by the outward physical appearance of the glass, but also by exhaustive fluorescence studies using examples of unquestionable Muranese attribution. Plate 196 illustrates one of several Venetian style glassware examples we have isolated which bear a script Moser signature. Claude V. Cox, in his book titled *Ludvig Moser, Royal Glass Artisan,* attributes this glass type to the Moser firm. In contrast, the large charger in Plate 197 is signed "Murano" in white enamel. Other examples of this glass have been found with their original Italian paper labels still intact. To further confuse the issue, there are no significant differences in the style of decoration, quality and mode of execution or glass types which could be used to isolate more than one supplier. Two possible explanations for this dichotomy come immediately to mind. Historically, Italy was a major consumer of Moser glass. Coupled with the established Moser tradition of purchasing glass blanks earmarked for the enameling studio, it is quite possible Muranese glass was purchased, decorated by Moser and subsequently marketed in Italy. Bohemian design influences notwithstanding, it is equally possible that Venetian style glassware was produced in its entirety by Muranese factories. While resolution of this problem may be of great importance to glass historians, it should be of little consequence to people who appreciate fine glass. Venetian style glassware manufactured prior to World War II is of consistently high quality, can be found in a wide range of decorative variations and should be considered highly collectable.

Large Floral Enameling

After 1900, delicately enameled floral forms, Baroque and Rococo themes and lavish gilding partially gave way to decorative motifs dominated by flowering plants executed on colored or shaded glass blanks. A probable outgrowth of the deeply engraved Art Nouveau style, enameled examples generally lack the sinuous lines characteristic of the fully developed Art Nouveau form (Plates 107, 140, 141 and 142). Floral enameled glass in this category was decorated by first outlining the major design elements with a mottled gold enamel (not to be confused with gilding or composite gold-enamel) and then fixing the enamel in a kiln; a second enameling and firing completed the decoration. This technique produced distinct boundaries between the outline and the shaded enamel filler. In addition to outlining, the gold-colored enamel was employed in many cases to provide a bouquet type backdrop for the main subject. Typical backdrops were composed of finely leafed foliage or "Baby's Breath." In most instances it appears as if the background was applied with the aid of a stencil. In terms of variety of color shading, size and general availability, vases decorated with enameled pansies (Plate 140) must have enjoyed a high level of popularity. At least five graded sizes, starting at a minimum height of 8 inches, were produced by Moser. We wish to point out that Legras & Cie (France) produced a line of enameled glass under the name "Mont Joye" which is similar to that just described. With the exception that Legras generally applied floral enameling to clear glass vessels of simple form, unsigned examples, unless carefully scrutinized, can easily be mistaken for Moser.

Ungilded Enamel on Glass

In this section we consider enameled subject matter which does not fall generically into the other decorative categories outlined in this chapter. Positive identification of Moser wares in this class, without the benefit of signed examples having similar or identical composition, is quite difficult. In some instances the style of enameling and/or glass form is sufficiently removed from the mainstream of identifiable Moser characteristics that one is fortunate if a generalized geographic point of origin can be isolated. A case in point is the enameled vase in Plate 109. In other cases, glass and enameled styles overlap those of other manufacturers, thus confusing proper attribution.

Production of ungilded enameled glass apparently dates to the earliest days of the Moser firm and most certainly encompasses an extensive variety of decorative styles, many of which have yet to be identified. Of the limited examples included in this book, several are worthy of further comment. Particular note should be taken of the effervescent white floral enameling present on the vases in Plate 6. From a historical design standpoint, this decorative style is strongly linked to the 19th-century Egermann urn pictured in Plate 1. Plate 153 represents a typical Bohemian decorative form produced by many glasshouses throughout the 19th century. Tableware decorated in this style was pictured in Moser catalogs of the 1920's. Enameled decoration on the 20th-century examples in Plates 199 and 200 is essentially a direct copy of a pattern present on 16th-or 17th-century Spanish glass. As a general rule, this type of decoration was applied to Venetian style tableware and is occasionally found bearing a Moser script signature. Plate 143 illustrates a decanter and two vases which, because of their distinctive flamboyant enameling, have been included in this section. Examples of this type emphasize whimsical themes, are typically signed in gold by the artist and were produced by Moser in the early 1920's. From the decorative themes employed, it seems likely that glassware of the type pictured in Plates 199, 200 and 143 was primarily intended for the Spanish market.

Within the general category of enameled glass, examples marketed by Thomas Webb & Sons, England, most closely resemble those produced by Moser. Webb enameling was internationally recognized for its exquisite beauty; floral bouquets with birds and insects, primarily butterflies, executed in vibrant colors were a specialty. Combining these features with the use of quality glass and finishing techniques, gilded bands and rims, and enameled beading in the Bohemian style, makes it quite easy to confuse enameled wares manufactured by Moser and Webb. A major point of differentiation, however, is the type of glass blanks to which the enameled decoration was applied.

As a general rule, Webb enameling is found on opaque colored glass (often referred to as "Bristol type") or shaded glass having an opaque white interior casing. Moser enameling, on the other hand, is typically associated with transparent colored glass. Plates 106 and 136 are examples of Moser floral enameling which is quite similar to that executed by Webb.

C. MOLDED GLASS

It was not uncommon for major glasshouses of the late 19th and early 20th centuries to market molded glass items as an adjunct to their premium lines of artistic glass. In the eyes of numerous collectors, the recognition of molded glassware is eclipsed by the more glamorous and expensive art glass forms. However, it must be remembered that molded glass not only permitted the acquisition of artistically designed glass by those of lesser financial means, but also, in many instances, provided much of the monetary support required for more aesthetic endeavors. At what point in time the Moser factory at Meierhöfen commenced production of molded glass forms remains undefined. It is recorded that Moser marketed molded glass designed by Josef Hoffman prior to World War I. Judging from its relative availability, it appears likely that molded glassware initially represented but a small fraction of Moser's total artistic glass output. With the advent of the Great Depression, however, financial pressures to greatly reduce fabrication costs naturally increased the importance of molded artistic glass and led to the introduction of finely executed designs typified by the examples illustrated in Plates 205 and 206.

CHAPTER V, Selected References:
Moser, Leo, "Commercial Art Glass," *The Glass Industry,* March 1942 (New York). Kreidl, Norbert J., "Rare Earths," *Journal of the American Ceramic Society,* Vol. 25 (1942), pp. 141-143. Českísklo, XIX stoleti, Moravska Galerie V, Brnê, Červen-Žaî, 1979. Neuwirth, Waltraud, *Orientalisierende Gläser, J.&L. Lobmeyr, Band 1.* Wien: Selbstverlag Dr. Waltraud Neuwirth, 1981; and *Wiener Werkstätte,* Wien: Selbstverlag Dr. Waltraud Neuwirth, 1984. Mackay, James, *Dictionary of Turn of the Century Antiques,* London: Wardlock Limited, 1974. Mundt, Barbara, *Historismus,* Berlin, 1974. Pazaurek, Gustav E., and Walter Spiegl, *Glas des 20. Jahrhunderts, Jugendstil-Art Déco,* München: Klinkhardt & Biemann, 1983. Arwas, Victor, *Glass-Art Nouveau to Art Deco,* New York: Rizzoli Int. Pub. Inc., 1980. Pattern books, catalog segments and melt journals related to Moser production from 1919 to 1933 are retained by the Corning Museum of Glass.

VI. MOSER GLASSES AND FABRICATION TECHNIQUES

Artistic style and decorative execution are but one side of the coin in establishing the value of artistic glass. Without the basis afforded by technical excellence in glass refining, forming and finishing techniques, the finest artistic efforts would be like singing Verdi's "Aida" accompanied by the strident tones of a honky-tonk piano.* Just as the technical characteristics indigenous to a particular glass manufacturer have the ability to reinforce overall quality, these same characteristics can ofttimes provide valuable clues as to the proper attribution of unsigned examples. In addition to the obvious properties of color, purity, weight and finishing techniques, fluorescence, induced by ultraviolet radiation, adds an important dimension to the study of glass. While the use of fluorescence to attribute glass to a specific manufacturer remains largely unexplored territory, its value in differentiating between glass types, determining the structural configuration of a glass sample, disclosing the presence of chemical stains or conditioning agents (i.e., prior to the application of gold, etc.), or isolating repairs, is well established.

Prior to 1892, Moser functioned solely as a glass decorating firm, purchasing glass blanks from suppliers located throughout Bohemia. Within this logistic framework, acquiring particular glass colors and shapes of acceptable quality over a prolonged time period, such as would be required to market and support the sale of extensive multifunctional tableware sets, would have been extremely difficult, if not impossible. It was probably this consideration more than any other which drove Ludwig Moser to establish his own glass furnaces.

In contrast to the cut and engraved crystal which dominated Moser table service designs, enameled glassware was generally reserved for decorative or less utilitarian objects. The aesthetic appearance of moderately to heavily enameled glass is less dependent on glass quality (bubbles, stria, etc.) and nuances in color than engraved, cut or lightly gilded glass. Consequently, it appears that a significant portion of the enameled glass Moser marketed after 1895 continued to employ glass blanks purchased from outside suppliers, in particular from Meyr's Neffe's Adolf works in Winterberg. With Moser's purchase of the Adolf works in 1922, the production of enameled glassware was apparently moved to that facility, where it remained until 1933 when the Adolf works was sold.

When the glass furnaces at Meierhöfen became operational in 1895, the Moser firm concentrated on the development and production of high quality crystal. Throughout its history, the Meierhöfen facility never wavered in its dedication to the production of the highest-purity crystal or to the execution of cut and engraved designs which emphasized the gem-like quality of the crystal mass. With its opening, Ludwig Moser initiated an experimental program directed at improving the quality of existing formulations as well as developing new types of glass. A direct result of this initiative was the early introduction of new glass colors: rich shades of dark ruby, dark cobalt blue, emerald green and amethyst mauve. In shaded variants, these new colors formed the basis of the deeply engraved Art Nouveau glass for which Moser became justifiably famous. Moser also produced a little-known form of rainbow colored glass primarily composed of striated blue, yellow and pink glass; green and opaque white has also been reported. Rather than being a glass mixture, rainbow glass was constructed by the careful additon of colored glasses to a clear gather prior to expanding it to its final dimensions (Plate 130). Cased and enameled versions of rainbow glass are considered rare. After 1921, Beryl, a lovely turquoise colored glass obtained by using Ce-Ti yellow glass modified with Cu (Plate 164), and Eldor, a pure lemon-yellow representing glass gold (Plate 169), were introduced. Of primary significance, however, was

---

*In using the term "glass refining," we are here referring to chemical purity.

the development of rare-earth doped glasses of which Alexandrit, Heliolit and Royalit are typical. Plates 177 and 178 present a partial palette of unique, highly refined Moser glasses developed primarily for Modern and Art Deco cutting styles; additional glass samples are in the possession of the Corning Museum of Glass.

Table II lists the non-rare-earth glasses given in the factory melt journal for which color samples are known to exist. These glasses represent only 37 types out of a total journal listing of 61. Most of the glasses listed in the melt journal from which this tabulation was derived were developed after World War I. They

TABLE II: NON-RARE EARTH MOSER GLASSES

Name	Color	Plate/Reference Source
Amethyst	deep amethyst	129
Beryl	pale aqua	164,177
D. W. Blau	moderate density bright blue	177
Giftgrün	moderate density green-aqua	177
Gold Topaz	gold amber	178
Lavendblau (dated 12/2/30)	moderate density lavender-blue	177
Lichtbryl (dated 11/10/30)	very pale aqua	177
L. W. Altgrün (dated 1/16/30)	moderate density olive-green	178
Lmaragd	deep sea-green	Corning
Oliv	pale olive-green	178
Ozeangrün	moderate density ocean-green	178
Proles (several examples bearing the same designation)	moderate density brown-amber lavender-brown lavender-pink	Corning
Radion	brilliant greenish-yellow	Corning
Ranchrot Light	moderate density pinkish-brown	Corning
Ranchroth	moderate density pinkish-brown	Corning
Ranchtopaz	moderate density gray-brown	Corning
Ruby (dated 4/12/29)	moderate density ruby-red	177
Rossgrün	brownish-amber	178
Stahlblaü	moderate density bright blue	Corning
Saphir	moderate density sapphire-blue	Corning
Weinroth	pale lavender-pink	Corning
W89	light pinkish-brown	177

can be found free formed, cut or engraved; however, they are rarely found bearing enameled decoration.

After 1920, several variations of lead crystal were developed by the Moser firm. Although examples of this glass are easily found (Plates 182 and 194), when the emphasis shifted from colored to clear crystal around 1930, Moser production remained dominated by Bohemian crystal. Moser advertisements of the period actually emphasized the weight saving to be realized by using Bohemian crystal in place of lead crystal.

Lower to moderate color density glasses, such as those listed in Table II, were normally used in a homogeneous form (i.e., constant color throughout the glass thickness) to create a particular object. If a lighter or graduated shading was desired, the final glass blank would typically be of cased construction.

Fabrication of cased glass is not only technically challenging and costly but requires considerable glass-blowing skill to produce high quality examples. A particularly critical area in the fabrication of cased glass occurs when two glasses having different thermal expansion coefficients are fused together at a high temperature. If the difference in expansion coefficients is sufficiently great, stress created at the boundary layer between the two glasses during the cooling process will produce fracturing. One technique which is quite useful in joining glasses with widely differing expansion coefficients is to sandwich a thin layer of glass, having an intermediate expansion coefficient, between the two primary glasses. With this transition layer, which we refer to as an expansion-matching layer, loss due to stress-induced fracture is much less likely to occur. Typically, intermediate glass layers of this type are only several thousandths of an inch thick. Establishing their presence requires the use of a short-wavelength ultraviolet lamp and clear access to a cross-sectional area of the glass sample.

Ruby colored glass, which in its paler shades is sometimes referred to as cranberry glass, was probably the most popular glass produced by Bohemian glass-houses. With comparatively few exceptions, such as the homogeneous deep ruby glass produced at Meier-höfen (Plates 170 and 177) or Venetian style ruby glass, shaded and solid color ruby glass marketed by Moser was of cased construction. The trumpet vase in Plate 13, probably decorated at Meistersdorf, consists of five layers of glass; progressing from the exterior toward the interior there is a heavy clear glass layer, an expansion-matching layer, a relatively thick casing of ruby glass, a second expansion-matching layer and a final casing of protective clear glass. Plate 118 illustrates an Art Nouveau goblet manufactured at Meierhöfen which is of rather unusual construction; thick pale ruby glass was used as the outer layer for both the bowl and foot, the interior of the bowl was cased with a thin layer of clear crystal and the two interior layers of the foot were alternately constructed from clear and ruby glass. As a general rule, ruby or cranberry glass was fabricated using a three-layer casing consisting of a thick clear exterior glass, a thin ruby-glass layer and a thin clear glass protective inner layer.

Several additional glass types are of particular interest. Bohemian variegated lemon-yellow glass, for example, is constructed from three or four cased layers. The outer three layers, which, as one pro-gresses toward the interior, are clear, clear streaked with opaque-white, and lemon-yellow, are of approxi-mately equal thickness. A thin glass layer, only visible under short-wavelength ultraviolet radiation, was sometimes applied over the lemon-yellow glass. Shaded pale pink-amber to apple-green glass, believed to have been made at Meierhöfen and illustrated in Plate 129, exhibits two cased layers of approximately equal thickness when viewed from the green end. Examples of deeply engraved Art Nouveau glass, in the shaded variants clear-amethyst, clear-green and clear-blue (Plates 112, 113 and 114), reveal the pres-ence of five cased layers. A clear crystal outer layer, on which the engraved decoration was worked, comprises 90 to 95% of the total glass thickness. With the exception that the colored layer is comparatively thin for these glasses, cased construction follows that of the trumpet vase (Plate 13) previously described. Color shading in glass is generally produced by varying the thickness of the colored layer. Two such graduated layers, joined to maintain a constant wall thickness, were used to produce the double-shaded Art Nouveau vase in Plate 117. Plate 119 illustrates a similar double-shaded vase which exhibits the added complexity of having a thin clear glass protective layer, on both the exterior and interior vessel surfaces, which decreases in thickness as the thickness of the colored layer decreases. Excluding Amberina glass (Plate 90), which was colored by a reheating process, the remaining shaded glasses marketed by Moser were generally fabricated from a minimum of three cased layers. Where available, specific construction details are included with the photographic plate descriptive information.

SUMMARY OF DISTINCTIVE CHARACTERISTICS

Included below is a compilation of technical and distinctive characteristics associated with Moser glass. Some of these are typical of high quality Bohemian glass in general, while others are more intimately associated with Moser glass in particular. Venetian style glassware is unique and quite different from other types of Moser related glasses; typical characteristics indigenous to this glass type are listed separately.

Mainstream Moser Glassware

* Concave polished pontil mark or flat polished base; exceptions include mold-blown and formed articles not requiring the use of a pontil rod.
* Double chamfered rim (both edges); exceptions are fire-polished rims (rarely ,used) or articles with applied rim decoration.
* Gilded rim (not a unique Moser characteristic); exceptions, deeply engraved Art Nouveau, Modern, Art Deco and German neo-Renaissance glass.
* Extensive use of mold-blown paneled glass for enamel-decorated ware.
* Generally heavyweight crystal; however, on a per volume basis, clear Moser crystal is considerably lighter than most contemporary crystal due to the absence of lead in the melt.

* Lavish use of gilding (both silver and gold) when appropriate to the style of an article.
* Shaded and ruby glass is generally constructed from three to five cased layers.
* Limited use of lead crystal; no known examples prior to 1918.
* After 1895, glass intended for cut or engraved decoration is of flawless quality.
* Facet and panel cutting executed with high mechanical precision.

Venetian Style Glassware

* Rough but recessed pontil marks from solid pontil rods.
* Folded-under foot construction.
* Applied circular glass rims on plates and bowls.
* Lightweight glass.
* Fire-polished rims.
* Gilded rims generally applied only on dark colored glasses.
* Highly refined glasses in deep rich tones of ruby, cobalt blue and green, as well as light colored glasses, amber and blue being typical, which emulate early Venetian glass styles.

CHAPTER VI, Selected References:
Hájek Jindřich, "Karlovy Vary—The Cradle of the 'Glass of Kings,'" *Czech. Glass Review,* Vol. 2 (1964), p. 42. Melt journals listing the types of glass produced by Moser after 1916 reside at the Corning Museum of Glass. Glass construction was derived from detailed flourescence studies conducted by the authors.

VII. IDENTIFICATION AND DATING OF MOSER GLASS— A WORD OF CAUTION

To the collector of fine glass, the foremost criteria to be used in evaluating the intrinsic worth of a particular object should be artistic design and quality of execution. Fortunately, these characteristics can be easily assessed by a trained or discriminating observer. Rarity, factory of origin and date of manufacture, while also exerting a significant influence over the market value of a particular item, are generally more difficult to determine and require a considerable depth of knowledge to be placed in proper perspective. Rarity, perhaps the most illusive property of all, must ultimately be based on the number of items available to the collector. Incomplete factory records regarding production quantities, as well as natural attrition over the years, compel one to rely on the frequency with which a particular item appears on the open market to assess this property. Needless to say, such an approach is fraught with difficulties and inaccuracy, and one can indeed find oneself treading a fine line by declaring a particular form to be rare. Articles of glass which can be attributed to a specific manufacturer are of extreme importance to a glass historian and, in the case of signed examples, can substantially influence market value. One must be careful, however, not to lose sight of the artistic significance of a piece in deference to its possessing an identifiable signature. Quality, more than any other factor, should remain of paramount importance in determining ultimate value.

Bohemia is composed of a geographically isolated land area approximately the size of Pennsylvania. Within its confines, the 19th and early 20th centuries witnessed what was perhaps the greatest concentration of manufacturers engaged in the production of artistic glass to be found anywhere in the world. Since much of the artistic glass produced in Central Europe was never signed, it is little wonder that associating artistic styles to specific firms or evaluating the extent to which rival Bohemian glasshouses adopted each other's profitable product lines presents a formidable task. Problems of this nature can be appreciated by considering a microcosm of the glass industry which existed in the Haida-Steinschönau region of northern Bohemia.* Although decorating workshops were associated with many major glass manufacturing houses, a considerable portion of their raw glass output was distributed by independent glass dealers to local groups of "home workers." These groups would, in turn, be responsible for decorating the glass and returning it to the dealers for marketing. Home worker organizations rarely exceeded 15 members, yet, in 1900, it is recorded that over 60% of the total number of glass decorators employed in the Haida-Steinschönau area fell under this classification. Complementing this extensive home industry were major glass decorating firms which, within the 1900-1930 time frame, included such names as Beyermann & Co. (Haida), Conrath & Liebsch (Steinschönau), Carl Goldberg (Haida), Hartmann & Dieterichs (Haida), Carl Hosch (Haida), W. Kulka (Haida), Gebr. Lorenz (Steinschönau), Carl Meltzer & Co. (Langenau), Julius Mülhaus & Co. (Haida), Joh. Oertel & Co. (Haida), Gebr. Pallme König (Steinschönau), Friedrich Pietsch (Steinschönau), Brüder Rachmann (Haida), Carl Schappel (Haida) and Tschernich & Co. (Haida).

In spite of the complexity of the Bohemian art glass industry, articles produced by the Moser firm are of a sufficiently distinctive character that proper attribution is possible for a reasonable percentage of the examples encountered. A few of the more notable exceptions include German neo-Renaissance glass, ungilded-enameled glass and engraved glass which, without the benefit of a reliable signature, can be extremely difficult to associate with a specific source. Glassware decorated in the Acanthus Ornamentation style is known to have been marketed concurrently by J.&L. Lobmeyr/Meyr's Neffe, Moser and, perhaps, several additional Bohemian firms. There is little doubt, however, that glassware decorated in the style

---

*Moser's Meistersdorf decorating facility was located within this geographical area.

illustrated in Plate 30, which is generally attributed to Moser by American collectors, was actually produced at Meyr's Neffe's Adolf works.

Graf Harrach in Neuwelt (Nový Svêt) was a major producer of engraved Art Nouveau glass quite similar to that produced by Moser. Plate 121 compares two engraved Art Nouveau vases of Moser and Harrach origin. Both of these vases are of similar heavyweight construction; however, close comparison reveals several distinctive differences. In contrast to the gradual shading of clear to amethyst (bottom to top) exhibited by the Moser vase, the Harrach example shades from a deeper amethyst to clear with a rather abrupt change in shading. Engraving on the Moser vase is considerably deeper than on its Harrach counterpart, and, in general, Moser engraved forms are proportionally larger in scale than those employed by Harrach. Plate 122 illustrates a Harrach engraved Art Nouveau vase with gilded highlights. At present, the Art Nouveau style of gold-enamel decoration employed on the Harrach vases pictured in this book appears to be a distinctive characteristic of Harrach production. In addition to the fact that Harrach produced engraved Art Nouveau glass in the style introduced by Moser, it has been brought to our attention that enameled pansy vases, similar to those pictured in Plate 140, were also marketed by that firm.

With the notable exception of Alexandrit, the majority of rare-earth doped glasses introduced and manufactured by Moser remain unique in the world of artistic glass. In the United States, the A.H. Heisey Glass Co. produced a glass which cannot be distinguished from Alexandrit when viewed under tungsten or fluorescent ambient lighting. Fortunately, it appears that a high percentage of Moser Alexandrit was signed, which, in conjunction with its principal use for Modern and Art Deco style art glass, aids considerably in establishing a proper attribution.

Prior to World War I, Meyr's Neffe was a significant contributor to the field of Bohemian artistic glass; yet, Meyr's Neffe remains a virtual unknown among American collectors. This lack of recognition can largely be attributed to the fact that a major portion of the artistic glass produced at Meyr's Neffe's Adolf works was actually marketed in the United States by the Viennese based firm of J.&.L. Lobmeyr. By the 1880's, J.&.L. Lobmeyr had developed into the foremost glass merchandising organization in Europe, but, due to inadequate manufacturing facilities and a shortage of glass decorators in the Vienna area, was dependent for its survival on an extensive network of design and production facilities situated throughout Austria and Bohemia. In addition to a permanent staff of designers, Lobmeyr commissioned original works from Central European artists and design groups which were subsequently executed by Bohemian factories. The necessity of a close liaison with Bohemian factories is attested to by the fact that when Austria and Bohemia were separated in 1918, Stefan Rath, the acting director of J.&.L. Lobmeyr prior to World War I, left Vienna to found a glass works, the J.&.L. Lobmeyr's Neffe Stefan Rath, in Steinschönau.

When Ludwig Lobmeyr engaged Meyr's Neffe to produce Renaissance type glassware in the late 1860's, Ludwig Moser represented a comparatively unrecognized portion of the Bohemian artistic glass industry. With the opening of the Meistersdorf refinery, this situation was dramatically altered. By the middle 1870's Moser glass had gained international prominence and, with Ludwig Moser's subsequent appointment as supplier to the Austrian Imperial Court, rose to a preeminent position with respect to rival Bohemian glasshouses. With these developments, the marketing acumen of Ludwig Lobmeyr would have required the consideration of Moser as a potential supplier of artistic glass to the Lobmeyr firm. An additional and possibly consequential factor was the timely marriage of Ludwig Moser to Julie Meyer. Even in the face of these intriguing circumstances, evidence suggests that Moser and Lobmeyr remained competitors until Moser purchased Meyr's Neffe's Adolf works in 1922. After that, Lobmeyr apparently continued to market glass produced at the Adolf works. Occasionally, one finds glassware dating from this later period which is co-signed "Moser and Lobmeyr." Plate 167 illustrates a co-signed engraved goblet originally designed by Stefan Rath and belonging to Lobmeyr's table set no. 253. A distinctive Moser 19th-century decorative style is quite evident on the tumbler in Plate 188; however, this example bears a gold Lobmeyr signature and was probably produced at the Adolf works after 1921.

Source identification and date of manufacturer are both required to establish the provenance of a particular article. Clues to the dating of artistic glass can originate from a multiplicity of sources. Factory records and catalogs provide irrefutable proof of provenance but are in many instances either missing completely or at best reveal only fragmentary information. Factory marks and artist signatures, while providing valuable evidence, require specialized knowledge for proper attribution, which can only be confirmed through historic records. Stylistic epochs, such as the Second Rococo and Biedermeier, and their associated glass types and forms, cutting and engraving styles and decorative motifs represent the front line of attack in dating examples for which no documented evidence exists.

Glass types and forms employed by Moser prior to the opening of the Meierhöfen works are of little use in dating since they were acquired from various factories located throughout Bohemia. Further, the characteristic Bohemian intransigence in the face of changing world styles was exemplified by early Moser production. Adherence to traditional Biedermeier and Second Rococo/Bohemian Baroque decorative themes, even after the remainder of the Bohemian artistic glass industry had shifted to more progressive forms, was characteristic of Moser glass. Indeed, many of these themes remained popular into the 20th century and were utilized in various forms up until World War II. Even though Moser glass produced during the latter half of the 19th century was distinctive, accurate dating is complicated by the longevity of many of the decorative themes employed. Fortunately, a rather complete set of Moser factory records for the 1910-1933 period were brought to the United States by Leo Moser.* Although only covering articles produced at the Meierhöfen works, these papers provide us with extensive documentation regarding glass types, forms and cutting styles produced during this period. Additional insight into the production of Art Nouveau forms at Meierhöfen can be obtained from various published works. With the interesting exception of enameled glassware, artistic glass production at Meierhöfen appears to be reasonably well defined.

*Moser factory records reside at the Corning Museum of Glass, Corning, New York.

Enameled glassware produced by the Moser firm remains an enigma. Of the Moser glass available to American collectors, enameled ware represents a significant portion; yet, there is almost a complete lack of recognition of Moser enameled glass in German and Czechoslovakian books and periodicals. There is essentially no reference to enameled glass in the Moser factory records during the tenure of Leo Moser as artistic director. Even though enameled glass was still being produced by Moser after 1930, eyewitness accounts indicate that this type of glass was absent from the major Moser showrooms in the Karlsbad area as well as from the main factory showroom at Meierhöfen. From available evidence, we have concluded that beginning with World War I, and most probably well before that time, the majority of enameled glass produced by the Moser firm was exported to countries outside of the Central European area. This factor, in conjunction with a merchandising policy that emphasized the production of specialized glassware for widely divergent geographical areas, significantly complicates the accurate dating of enameled glass.

For the reader's convenience, we have included a tabulated aid for dating Moser glass. In using this table, it must be recognized that the time frame specified for a particular identifying feature is only approximate and that in some isolated cases articles bearing this feature may actually have been produced at a time considerably at variance with that stated.

TABLE III: DATING AIDS TO MOSER GLASS PRODUCTION

1857-1862 Production was almost exclusively engraved or cut glass.

1862-1870 Some enameled glass produced; emphasis still on engraved glass.

1857-1875 Biedermeier designs produced.

1857-1900 Second Rococo/Bohemian Baroque style dominated Moser production. Forms of this style continued to be produced well after World War I.

1857-1895 Hunting and woodland scenes were popular themes for engraving.

1857-1900   Moser glass cutting styles emphasized panel faceting, flute and mitre cutting and raised oval panels (cabochons).

1870-1880   Production of Muslin glass.

1870-1890   Production of German neo-Renaissance glass.

1870-1895   Production of intricately detailed and lavishly decorated glassware based on Second Rococo/Bohemian Baroque and naturalistic themes.

1875-1885   Islamic, Chinese and Japanese style glass produced.

1875-1914   Production of iridescent glass.

1880-1895   Mary Gregory style decoration produced.

1885-1938   Wheel-cut and acid cut-back cameo forms; wheel-cut variant probably only produced during the 1885-1895 time frame; cameo in style of late Gallé and Daum (Nancy) produced around 1900; Amazon warrior frieze introduced about 1914.

1895-1910   Deeply engraved Art Nouveau and enameled Art Nouveau floral forms.

1895-1938   Colored and clear crystal production at Meierhöfen emphasized perfection of the crystal mass.

1895-1938   Clear crystal production dominated by Bohemian Crystal. Lead crystal was manufactured in limited quantities after 1920.

1900-1905   Karlsbader Secession glass produced.

1910-1938   Modern style cutting techniques employed.

1910-1938   Art Deco designs produced.

1910-1938   Large floral enameling forms produced.

1910-1938   Wiener Werkstätte designs produced.

1910-1938   Enameled glass reflected earlier themes but with modern overtones.

1914-1938   Production of molded artistic glass.

1922-1938   Rare-earth doped glasses produced.

1925-1938   Venetian style glassware appeared on market.

1930-1938   Production at Meierhöfen was primarily clear Bohemian Crystal.

CHAPTER VII, Selected References:
Weiss, Gustav, *The Book of Glass,* Praeger Publishing Co., 1971.

VIII. FACTORY MARKS

Through the years, Moser signatures have appeared in various guises. Many of the older factory marks persisted alongside newer varieties so that, with only a few exceptions, associating manufacturing dates with specific signatures can often prove misleading. A common thread linking the entire span of Moser production is a script signature (Figure 11) which ostensibly represents Ludwig Moser's personal signature. Appearing singularly or in combination with "Karlsbad," this signature is the one most often encountered by American collectors. In its singular form, the Moser signature is small in size, typically found nestled among the decorative elements of a particular example and is generally quite difficult to isolate. It is considerably less common to find the singular script signature on the base of an item than incorporated within the decorative motif.

Recently, the validity of the singular script Moser signature has been seriously questioned. Since this signature is generally scribed into the glass with a sharp instrument, the addition of spurious signatures by unscrupulous people is comparatively simple. However, the important question to be answered is whether this particular signature form was actually employed by the Moser factory in the first place. In arriving at a final conclusion, several factors must be considered: 1) If the initial purpose of introducing the script signature was to defraud, why place it within the decorative motif to obscure its presence?; 2) Within the authors' experience, few articles have been observed bearing the script signature which by themselves would not have been classified as Moser type; 3) Several examples have been found which simultaneously bear the script signature and their original paper labels; and 4) The validity and factory use of the script Moser signature has been confirmed by the Moser family. There seems little reason to doubt the authenticity of the script signature; however, one must be extremely careful not to base a Moser attribution exclusively on the presence of this signature form since fraudulent examples are known to exist.

Predominantly applied to glass articles during the 1895-1918 time frame, the signature illustrated in Figure 16 was adopted as the official trademark of the Moser firm and can be found on its business cards and catalogs. The addition of the two capital M's separated by a hock glass to the form in Figure 15 probably occurred when the Meierhöfen works opened in 1893-1895. Figuratively, this addition signifies the marriage of Ludwig Moser to Julie Meyer and, hence, the joining of two major Bohemian glassmaking families, Moser and Meyer.

In searching the Moser factory records we came across a series of cicular trademarks relating to Meyr's Neffe. The first of these, Figure 25, was employed prior to 1918, while the second, Figure 26, was probably used in the interim period of 1918 to 1922. Figure 27 appears to be a series of design samples under consideration after Moser purchased the Adolf works in 1922; Figure 27D was bracketed in the factory notes and may represent the design finally accepted for commercial use. We can be certain that the paper label in Figure 23 was employed as it was found on a free-blown Alexandrit bottle (Plate 165) which also bears the acid-etched signature in Figure 19. Figure 21 illustrates an important paper label employed by Moser prior to 1895. Of particular interest is the spelling of Karlsbad with an English "C" in place of the German "K". Articles bearing this label were probably manufactured for English or American export. Although signed Moser glass predating 1895 is comparatively rare, it is highly probable that most glass marketed before 1895 bore paper labels of this type.

Occasionally, one finds gilded, engraved or enameled numerals on the base of Moser glass. In the majority of cases, a series of gilded numbers was used to designate the basic glass form. These "form numbers" are found alone or in combination with a series of numerals which identify the decorative pattern, i.e., the series 2716/213, which appears on the amber juice glass in Plate 42, designates glass form #2716 and decorative pattern #213. During the production run of similar items requiring custom-fitted stoppers, the stoppers and base were often marked with identical one- or two-digit numbers to ensure proper mating of components. Additional numbers, apparently not falling into either of the above categories, are sometimes found; their purpose is presently undefined. Use of form numbers to estimate the earliest production date of a particular item does not appear to be reliable. Our research indicates that differing numerical series were employed prior to and after the opening of the Meierhöfen facility.

We close with a word of warning concerning the reliance on a signature to establish a Moser attribution.

Fraudulent Moser signatures, encompassing both the scribed and acid-etched forms, are an ever-present reality. Many of the examples bearing fraudulent signatures were actually marketed by the Moser firm, while others, primarily exhibiting poor quality workmanship, are of diverse origin. This problem is compounded by the fact that a multiplicity of signature forms were employed by the Moser firm and that new types are constantly being discovered. Signatures included in this book are of a more common variety but by no means represent a complete listing. It cannot be overemphasized that recognition of artistic and technical quality, in addition to a basic knowledge of the glass styles produced by a specific manufacturer is of paramount important in purchasing artistic glass. Absolute reliance on the presence of a signature can prove quite disappointing from both an aesthetic and a financial point of view.

Fig. 10   Comparison of signatures found on products of Lobmeyr and Meyr's Neffe. Left, common Lobmeyr signature in gold or enamel; used after 1860. Right, monogram employed by Meyr's Neffe.

Fig. 11   Singular script signature generally found incorporated within the design elements of a signed example; inscribed with the aid of a sharp instrument. Date of use covers pre-1870 to 1938.

Fig. 12   Early acid-etched signature; estimated dates of use are 1860-1870.

Fig. 13   Broad or fine line acid-etched signature; also found in enamel or scribed with a sharp instrument; estimated dates of use are 1870-1938.

MOSER

Fig. 14   Gilded signature; estimated dates of use are 1870-1895.

Fig. 15 Acid-etched signature appearing on items designated for export; estimated dates of use are 1891-1895.

Fig. 16 Acid-etched Moser trademark used from approximately 1895 to 1938; items designated for export incorporate "Made in Austria" prior to 1918 and "Made in Czechoslovakia" after 1918. Primary use as a signature on glass was in the 1895-1918 time frame.

Moser
TCHECO-
SLOVAQUIE

Fig. 17 Acid-etched signature; estimated date of use is 1918-1922.

Made in
Czechoslovakia
(Moser)

Fig. 18 Acid-etched signature used after 1918.

Moser

Moser

Moser

Fig. 19 Acid-etched signatures; estimated date of use is after 1920.

MOSER
KARLSBAD

CZECHO
SLOVAKIA

Fig. 20 Acid-etched Wiener Werkstatte/Moser
signature employed after 1922.

Fig. 21 Export paper label emblazoned with
the Habsburg Eagle; primarily employed prior
to 1890.

Fig. 22 Paper label employed after 1918.

Fig. 23 Meyr's Neffe paper label employed
after 1922.

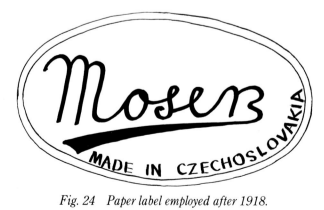

Fig. 24 Paper label employed after 1918.

Fig. 25 Design for Meyr's Neffe trademark used prior to 1918.

Fig. 26 Design for Meyr's Neffe trademark; estimated date, 1918-1922.

A.

B.

Fig. 27 Four Meyr's Neffe trademark designs for use after 1922.

C.

D.

IX. THE MAGIC OF MOSER

Historical background and technique development provide necessary ingredients for the full appreciation of fine artistic glass. In the final analysis, however, visual appeal has the last word in establishing the success or failure of a particular design. As one progresses through the following pages, the true magic of Moser dances before your eyes. From the earliest complex and intricate creations to the jewel-like simplicity of the Modern and Art Deco facet-cut styles, one cannot help but be impressed by the consistency of decorative balance and artistic execution. Unquestionably, visual appeal and Moser glass are synonymous terms.

Color plates presented in this chapter have been carefully selected to indicate the diversity in Moser production and organized chronologically to illustrate historical design development. Within this sampling we wish to highlight certain decorative features which, occurring chiefly on glass produced at Meistersdorf, are generally considered to be Moser trademarks: Tooled rims in combination with composite gold-enamel floral forms, Plate 10, or diaper-work, Plate 24; applied acorns with oak leaves, Plate 46; vermicular patterns executed in composite gold-enamel, Plates 35 & 47; adaptations of the Kakiemon porcelain rock-blossom motif, Plates 54, 55 & 56; applied grapes and grape leaves, Plate 63; composite gold-enamel swirls on a gilded ground, Plate 69 (an example, identical to that pictured, was presented by Ludwig Moser to the Smithsonian Institute in Washington, D.C.); brightly enameled leaves and seed pods in the pattern of Plate 76, and; the use of a stylized "H" design, Plate 98.

Attribution of the decanter in Plate 198 remains an open question. Its association with Pauly & Cia was established by comparing the decanter to a similar example which bore a Pauly & Cia paper label. It has recently been established, however, that beginning around 1900, and continuing after 1918, Pauly & Cia sold Moser glass throughout Italy under their own name. The example in Plate 198 may well have originated at Moser's Adolf works in Winterberg.

Plate 1

Plate 2

Plate 3

49

Plate 4

Plate 5

Plate 6

50

Plate 7

Plate 9

Plate 8

Plate 10

51

Plate 11

Plate 12

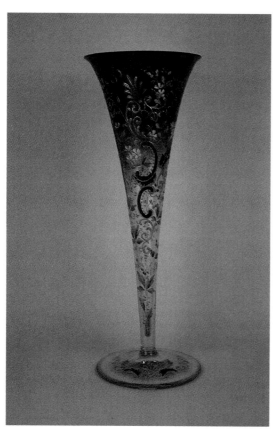

Plate 13

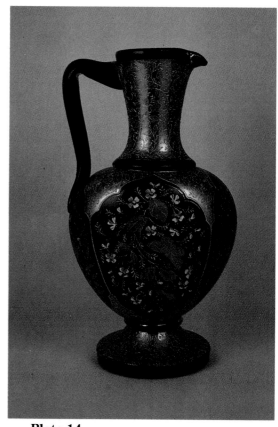

Plate 14

Plate 15

Plate 16

Plate 17

Plate 18

Plate 19

Plate 20

Plate 21

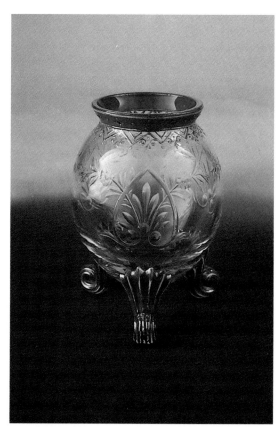

Plate 22

Plate 23

Plate 25

Plate 24

Plate 26

Plate 27

Plate 28

Plate 29

Plate 30

Plate 31

Plate 32

Plate 33

Plate 34

Plate 35

Plate 36

Plate 37

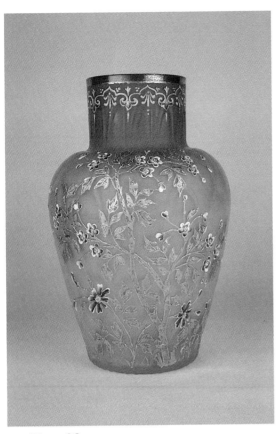

Plate 38

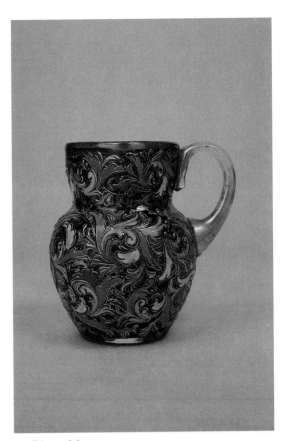

Plate 39

Plate 40

Plate 41

Plate 42

Plate 43

Plate 44

60

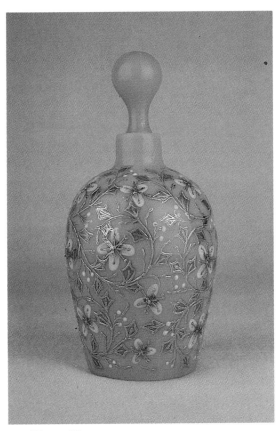

Plate 45

Plate 46

Plate 47

Plate 48

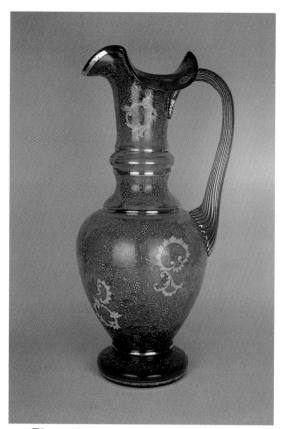

Plate 49

Plate 50

Plate 51

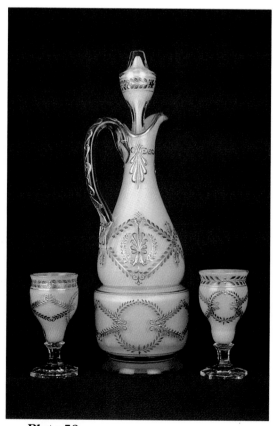

Plate 52

62

Plate 53

Plate 54

Plate 55

Plate 56

Plate 57

Plate 58

Plate 59

Plate 60

64

Plate 61

Plate 62

Plate 63

65

Plate 64

Plate 65

Plate 66

Plate 67

Plate 68

Plate 69

Plate 70

Plate 71

Plate 72

Plate 73

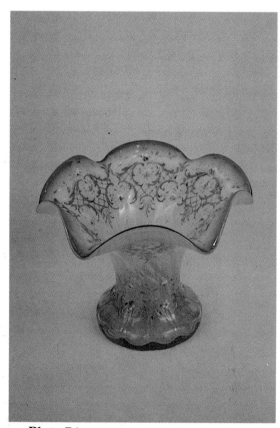

Plate 74

Plate 75

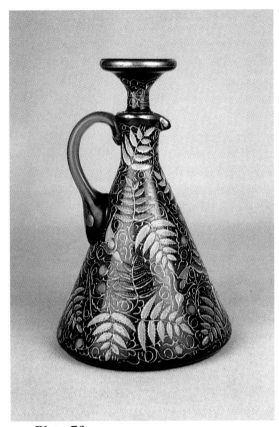

Plate 76

Plate 77

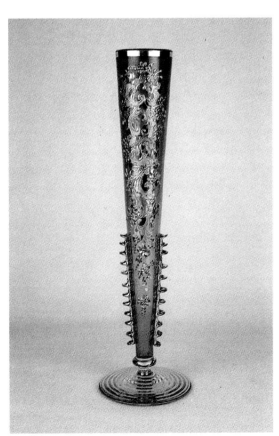

Plate 78

Plate 79

Plate 80

Plate 81

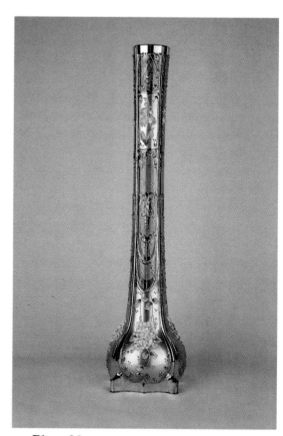

Plate 82

Plate 83

Plate 84

Plate 85A

Plate 85B

Plate 86

Plate 87

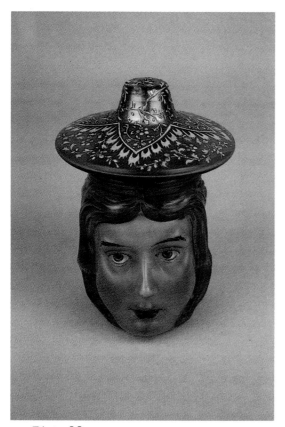

Plate 88

Plate 89

Plate 90

Plate 91

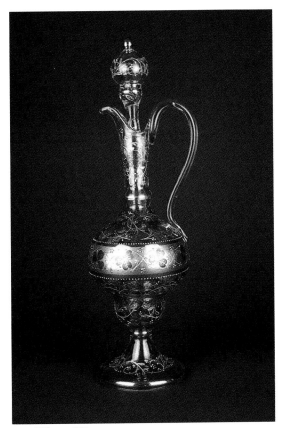

Plate 92

Plate 93

73

Plate 94

Plate 95

Plate 96

74

Plate 97

Plate 98

Plate 99

75

Plate 100

Plate 101

Plate 103

Plate 102

76

Plate 104

Plate 105

Plate 106

Plate 107

Plate 108

Plate 109

Plate 110

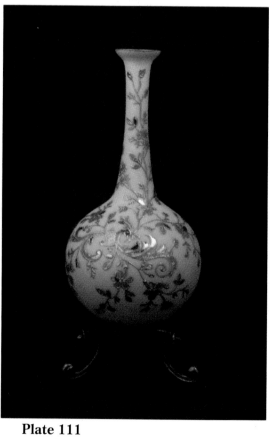

Plate 111

Plate 112

Plate 113

Plate 114

Plate 115

Plate 116

Plate 117

Plate 118

80

Plate 119

Plate 120

Plate 121

Plate 122

Plate 123

Plate 124

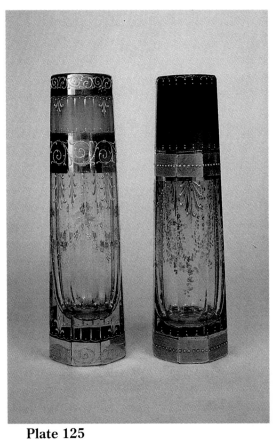

Plate 125

Plate 126

Plate 127

Plate 128

Plate 129

Plate 130

Plate 131

Plate 132

Plate 133

Plate 134

Plate 135

Plate 136

Plate 137

Plate 138

Plate 139

Plate 140

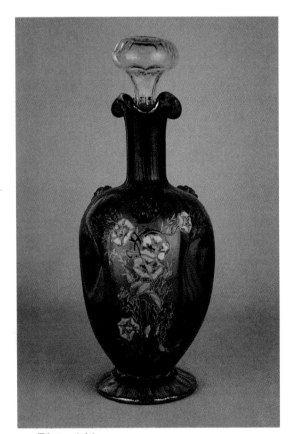

Plate 141

Plate 142

Plate 143

Plate 144

Plate 145

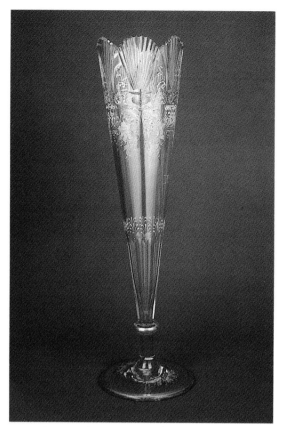

Plate 146

Plate 147

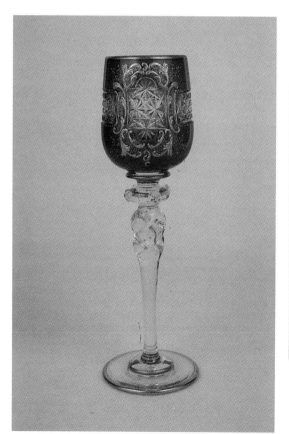

Plate 148

Plate 149

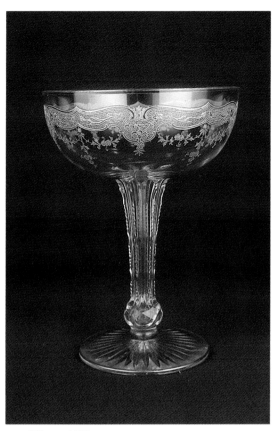

Plate 150

Plate 151

Plate 152

Plate 153

Plate 154

Plate 155

Plate 156

Plate 157

Plate 158

Plate 159

Plate 160

Plate 161

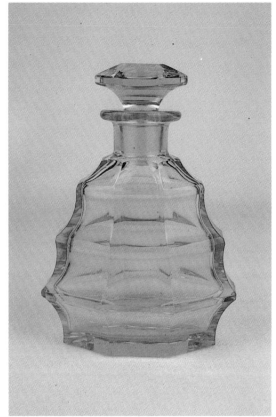

Plate 162

Plate 163

Plate 164

Plate 165

Plate 166

Plate 167

Plate 168

Plate 169

Plate 170

Plate 171

Plate 172

94

Plate 173

Plate 174

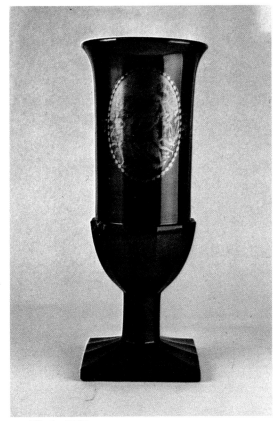

Plate 175

Plate 176

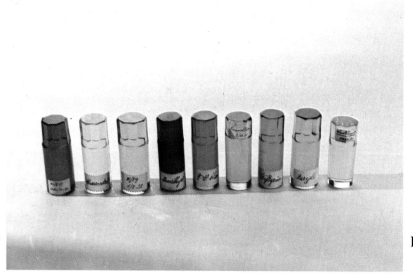

Plate 177

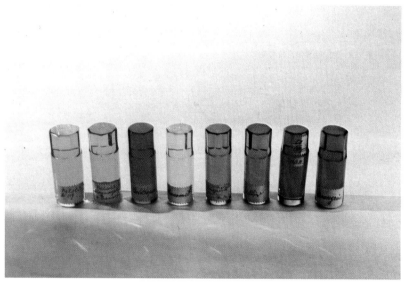

Plate 178

Plate 179

Plate 180

Plate 181

Plate 182

Plate 183

Plate 184

Plate 185

Plate 186

Plate 187

Plate 188

Plate 189

Plate 190

Plate 191

Plate 192

Plate 193

Plate 194

Plate 195

Plate 196

Plate 197

Plate 198

Plate 199

Plate 200

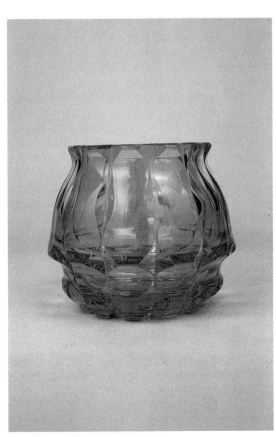

Plate 201

Plate 202

Plate 203

Plate 204

Plate 205

Plate 206

CAPTIONS

PLATE 1
Lidded urn in opaque satin-finished blue glass. From the studio of Friedrich Egermann. Attributed to the noted artist Alois Eiselt; Polevsko, near Ceská Lípa. Height 16½". c. 1815-1820.

PLATE 2
Biedermeier-style vase in three cased layers; blue to opaque-white to clear crystal. Attributed to Ludwig Moser. Height 9¼". c. 1860. Compliments of Mr. and Mrs. Harry Foreman.

PLATE 3
Disassembled amethyst and clear crystal Zwischengoldglas tumbler. Attributed to Ludwig Moser. Height 3¾". c. 1870. Compliments of Mr. and Mrs. Harry Foreman.

PLATE 4
Panel-cut lidded container of Biedermeier design in uranium-doped glass (Annagrün). Base is mitre-cut in a star and fan pattern. Each cabochon has a miniature enameled fruit, insect or flower surrounded by a foliate scroll cartouche. Body is decorated with gold and silver beading and trifoliate gold and enamel forms. Of possible Moser origin. Height 7½". c. 1840-1870.

PLATE 5
Early enameled clear-crystal grouping featuring translucent stained panels in shades of amber, blue, green, yellow and pink. Panels are bounded by mottled composite gold-enamel and contain enameled flowers and leaves in contrasting colors. Of possible Moser origin. Height of pitcher, 7⅝". c. 1870.

Plate 6
Mold-blown red-stained clear-crystal vases of Biedermeier form. Foliate decoration is executed in white and mustard-yellow enamels with subdued highlights. Central vase bears an acid etched "Moser Karlsbad" signature. Height 8½". c. 1860-1870.

PLATE 7
Two typical spa cups of possible Moser origin; c. 1870-1890. At left, handled mug with facet-cut panels; engraved woodland scene, name "Karlsbad" and measure graduations are gilded; height 5¼". At right, mold-blown tumbler decorated with enameled oak leaves and acorns; customized monogram in composite gold-enamel is on a silver shield; height 5".

PLATE 8
Two typical spa cups of possible Moser origin. At left, facet-cut oval cup with engraved scene of the Spradel Colonade-Karlsbad; height 4⅞". At right, clear-to-amethyst facet-cut oval cup in three cased layers; engraved with the name "Karlsbad"; height 5½". c. 1870-1890.

PLATE 9
Feline-form vase. Paneled blue glass body is decorated with brightly enameled and gilded floral and foliate scrolls; front legs, tail handle and rigaree collar are formed from amber glass. Of probable Moser origin. Height 7⅛". c. 1880.

PLATE 10
Dessert cup and underplate in a comparatively rare clear-to-blue glass; constructed from three cased layers. Gilded tooled rims and branch handles were a favorite Moser decorative form. Floral decorative motif is executed using composite gold-enamel. c. 1880.

PLATE 11
Shaded clear to emerald-green crystal constructed from five cased layers; c. 1880. Left to right, vase with engraved and gilded flowers with trailing vines; acid-etched signature "Moser Karlsbad"; height 6¼". Cologne bottle with engraved and gilded flowers, zipper cutting and gold-outlined facet-cut panels; acid-etched signature "Moser Karlsbad"; height 5⅝". Vase with engraved and gilded woodland scene; height 8⅜".

PLATE 12
Cranberry trifoil vase in three-layer cased glass. Alternating clear and gilded panels are decorated with composite gold-enamel scrollwork and enameled flowers. Signed in script, "Moser." Height 4". c. 1880.

PLATE 13
Rubina trumpet vase constructed from five cased layers. Composite gold-enamel Rococo scrolls, rocaille and palmettes are accented by enameled flowers and leaves; dark fill areas appear to be of metallic composition. Of probable Moser origin. Height 15¾". c. 1880.

PLATE 14
Large ewer in dark green glass. Opposing front and side panels are decorated with composite gold-enamel leaves, butterflies and enameled flowers; foot, neck and panel surround have composite gold-enamel floral scrolls on a comparatively rare silver ground. Height 12″. c. 1880.

PLATE 15
Paneled amber vase with blue lava rim and rigaree belt. Large enameled glass salamander has jeweled eyes. Floral enameled decoration is outlined in gold. Height 12″. c. 1880. Courtesy of Oscar Ghebelian.

PLATE 16
Clear-crystal mustard jar with enameled flowers and butterfly; silver-plated brass mounts. Signed in script, "Moser." Height 5″. c. 1880.

PLATE 17
Amber crackel-glass vase with applied prunts and drops. Two realistically enameled applied glass fish swim on a backdrop of enameled aquatic plants outlined in gold. Height 7″. c. 1880.

PLATE 18
Green cut-to-clear decanter set in three-layer cased glass; green panels on stopper are stained. Base of tray and decanter have radial mitre cuts with a fine gold line running along the apex of each cut. Face-cut areas surrounding each emerald cobochon are decorated with intricate composite gold-enamel Rococo scrollwork. Of probable Moser origin. Decanter is 11″ high; tray is 9¾″ in diameter. c. 1880.

PLATE 19
Traditional Bohemian varigated yellow glass comprised of four cased layers. c. 1890. Left to right, juice glass with finely executed band of composite gold-enamel scrollwork; signed in gold, "MOSER"; height 3⅞″. Decanter with composite gold-enamel scrollwork, palmettes and beading; height 8¼″. Narrow juice glass decorated with a band of composite gold-enamel scrolled branches; encased cinder near base is hidden by a gilded insect. Height 3⅞″.

PLATE 20
Lightweight apple-green footed bowl of trifoliate design. Interior of bowl has enameled flowers on a gilded ground. Signed in script, "Moser." Height 3⅛″. c. 1890.

PLATE 21
Cased alabaster and rosaline compote with brightly enameled oak leaves trimmed in composite gold-enamel and applied acorns. Height 3⅛″. c. 1880.

PLATE 22
Engraved crystal egg-shaped vase on gilded reeded feet with composite gold-enamel and simulated jeweled border. Height 3″. Signed in gold, "MOSER." c. 1880.

PLATE 23
This charming miniature compote is red-stained Bohemian crystal decorated in a characteristic Moser style. Height 3⅛″. c. 1880.

PLATE 24
Rubina compote with three-layer cased bowl and clear-crystal pedestal foot. Composite gold-enamel floral diaper-work and a tooled rim represent a commonly found decorative style. Bowl is 5½″ in diameter. c. 1880.

PLATE 25
Attractive rubina master salt with tooled and gilded rims. Bowl and underplate are of three-layer cased construction; foot and stem are clear crystal. Enameled roses, outlined in composite gold-enamel, in combination with composite gold-enamel foliate scroll-work complete the decorative motif. Height of footed bowl is 3⅝″. c. 1880.

PLATE 26
Römer with three-layer cased rubina bowl and clear crystal foot; applied prunts. Height 4″. c. 1880.

PLATE 27
Paneled clear-to-citrone decanter in three cased layers. Hollow stopper and body are decorated with composite gold-enameled flowers joined by diaper-work. Acid-etched signaure, "Moser Karlsbad." Height 9¾″. c. 1880.

PLATE 28
Water set with fish scale decoration; three-layer cased construction. Although glass of this type might be found bearing a Moser or Lobmeyr signature, it was probably manufactured at the Meyr's Neffe Adolf works. Height of pitcher, 9″. c. 1890.

PLATE 29
A particularly elegant cranberry decanter in three-

layer cased glass. Panels outlined in gold and beading contain brightly enameled foliate scrolls and flowers as well as a stylized cascading fountain and fern pattern. Surround has shadded enameled flowers and leaves on a dark bronze metallic ground. Attributed to Moser or Meyr's Neffe. Height 13″. c. 1880.

PLATE 30
Three-layer cased cranberry decanter of graceful design belonging to Lobmeyr's table set no. 81. Body is decorated with brightly enameled foliate scrolls, flowers and gilded fish scales in a classical Acanthus Ornamentation motif. Attributed to Meyr's Neffe. Height 10¼″. c. 1880.

PLATE 31
Islamic-style three-layer cased cranberry vase with composite gold/silver-enamel decoration. Height 10½″. c. 1880. Compliments of Mr. and Mrs. William Baker.

PLATE 32
Clear crystal decanter with applied blue glass flowers. Composite gold-enamel decorative pattern reflects Islamic design influences. Hollow stopper is probably original. Height 9⅛″. c. 1880.

PLATE 33
Islamic-style vase with pale green iridescence and composite gold-enamel decoration. Of probable Moser origin. Height 8¼″. c. 1880.

PLATE 34
Transparent enameling and a gilded ground are combined in this clear crystal goblet to create a decorative pattern strongly influenced by Islamic art forms. Height 3⅝″. c. 1880.

PLATE 35
Executed in green glass, this mounted pedestal vase displays a characteristic vermicular pattern in composite gold-enamel which strongly points to a Moser origin. Height 12⅝″. c. 1880.

PLATE 36
Pale olive decanter decorated with brightly enameled Acanthus scroll ornamentation and enameled cherub. Of probable Moser origin. Height 8½″. c. 1880.

PLATE 37
Cup and saucer of unusual form. Copper-blue glass is distinctively decorated in a characteristic Moser pattern. Signed in gold on foot of cup, "85/4 Decor 19." c. 1880.

PLATE 38
Quilted rubina-verde vase composed of three cased layers. Green shading is provided by uranium-doped glass; ruby shading is rosaline glass. Composite gold-enamel branches and leaves are gold filled. Of probable Moser origin. Height 7½″. c. 1880.

PLATE 39
Miniature cranberry square-topped pitcher in three-layer cased glass. High density composite gold-enamel foliate scrollwork is accented with brightly colored enamels. Height 4¼″. c. 1880.

PLATE 40
Bohemian crystal vases of this type were produced with a variety of intricate composite gold-enamel decorative motifs. Height 11⅝″. c. 1880.

PLATE 41
Perfume bottle with hollow stopper in clear paneled crystal. Composite gold-enamel foliate scrolls are combined with transparent enameled leaves and flowers to provide a most pleasing contrast. Height 4½″. c. 1880.

PLATE 42
A sampling of juice glasses here and in Plates 43 and 44 provides but a hint of the diversity in decoration which was a Moser trademark. c. 1880-1890. Left to right, clear crystal; brightly enameled grape leaves and insect accented in composite gold-enamel. Inverted thumbprint three-layer cased clear-to-aqua glass; vermicular composite gold-enamel decor with enameled floral groupings. Clear crystal with composite gold/silver-enamel flower and foliate scrolls. Paneled amber glass; opaque enameled panels are highlighted with scrolls and palmettes; signed in gold, "MOSER."

PLATE 43
More juice glasses. Left to right, three-layer cased cranberry glass; composite gold-enamel swirling vines; composite gold-enamel scrolls around rim represent a characteristic Moser design. Single-layer green glass; composite gold-enamel leaves and berries. Three-layer cased citrone glass with large composite gold-enamel foliate scrolls and silver grape

clusters. Three-layer cased cranberry glass; composite gold-enamel flowers and large scrolls.

PLATE 44

Some more juice glasses. Left to right, light blue-green glass; composite gold-enamel leaves, enameled flowers and insects. Three-layer cased cranberry glass; white and blue enameled flowers with composite gold-enamel branches. Clear crystal decorated with blue enameled flowers and composite gold-enamel branches. Yellow-green uranium-doped crystal; composite gold-enamel leaves, enameled flowers and insects.

PLATE 45

Opaque aqua glass was a traditional Bohemian favorite. This example is decorated in a typical Moser motif consisting of composite gold-enamel leaves and white enameled flowers. Height 5½". c. 1880.

PLATE 46

Peach Blow pitcher with opaque white liner and clear acid-etched outer casing provide a striking background for the traditional Moser oak leaves and applied acorns. Height 5". c. 1880.

PLATE 47

Although comparatively rare, Moser enameling, such as on this charming miniature pitcher, does occasionally occur on stained Bohemian crystal. Height 2¾". c. 1880.

PLATE 48

Gray-green footed beaker with brightly enameled oak leaves and insects outlined in composite gold-enamel. Applied glass acorns have a gilded husk and a silvered seed pod. Height 4¼". c. 1880.

PLATE 49

Large ewer in green glass with gilded reeded handle. Decorative motif consists of composite gold-enamel grapes and grape leaves with enameled rocaille highlights. Height 15⅜". c. 1880.

PLATE 50

Copper-blue glass pitcher decorated with an enameled winter woodland scene. Decorative style points to a Moser origin. Height 10½". c. 1880.

PLATE 51

Left and right, a pair of green glass footed salts brightly enameled in the German neo-Renaissance style; these examples were purchased directly from the Moser factory in the early 1880's; height 2¾". Center, a matching pillbox. c. 1880.

PLATE 52

Clear crystal over opaque-white cased decanter set. Gold over enamel decoration is executed in the French Empire style. Signed in gold on base of decanter, "Moser Karlsbad." Height of decanter is 9". c. 1880.

PLATE 53

Rubina finger bowl and underplate in three-layer cased glass. Heavily executed composite gold-enamel foliate scrolls and fine floral forms provide an interesting and attractive contrast. Diameter of underplate, 6½". c. 1880.

PLATE 54

Clear crystal decanter (sans stopper) gilded and enameled in style similar to Japanese Kakiemon porcelain rock-blossom motif. Engraved signature, "Moser." Height 7½". c. 1880. Compliments of Mr. and Mrs. Richard Parsons.

PLATE 55

Doughnut-shaped decanter in olive-green glass; central hole has been cut and polished. Enameled and composite gold-enamel pattern is derived from the Japanese Kakiemon rock-blossom motif. Height 12½". c. 1880.

PLATE 56

Green glass vase on gilded brass mounts. Enameled decoration is a high density adaptation of the Kakiemon-derived motif pictured in Plate 54. Height 8¼". c. 1880.

PLATE 57

Three-layer cased cranberry vase featuring a gilded ground covered with brightly enameled flowers and leaves. Height 4½". c. 1880.

PLATE 58

Rubina cup and saucer in three-layer cased glass. Intricately executed white enameled scrolls, palmettes and beading are combined in an outstanding example of Moser enameled tableware. Signed in script, "Moser." Saucer is 4⅝" across flats. c. 1880.

PLATE 59

Unusual paneled vase in clear crystal with oven-worked rigaree handle and acorns. Gold signature, "MOSER." Height 7½". c. 1890.

PLATE 60

Opalescent glass vase with gilded applied feet. Enameled insect, flowers and leaves are outlined in a composite gold-orange enamel. Height 5". c. 1880.

PLATE 61

Amber vase formed from blown-out crackel glass to resemble a tree trunk. Applied and gilded blue glass lava base, vine and leaves provide added realism. No less than six applied and enameled glass insects complete a naturalistic motif which is characteristically Moser. Height 6⅝". c. 1880.

PLATE 62

Mold-blown amber glass vase with realistically enameled fish and aquatic plants. Height 8½". c. 1890.

PLATE 63

Green glass water set with brightly enameled grape leaves outlined in composite gold-enamel. Each glass has four clusters of applied grapes in yellow, blue, red and green glass. Glasses are 5⅜" high; tray is 11½" in diameter. c. 1880.

PLATE 64

Cordial decanter in green glass of typical Central European design; mounts are gilded brass. Composite gold-enamel decorative floral pattern points to a Moser origin. (Several hooks and glasses are missing from this example.) Height 10⅞". c. 1880.

PLATE 65

Large three-layer cased cranberry powder box with gilded brass mounts. Composite gold-enamel scroll-work, palmettes and a central medallion combined with applied jewels and high-relief floral enameling produce a most striking tour de force. Box is 10" in diameter by 6" high. c. 1880.

PLATE 66

Rubina cased and facet-cut vase. Gilded and silvered panels, enameled flowers, applied red and white jewels and composite gold-enamel scrollwork and beading create an intricate and attractive design. Of probable Moser origin. Height 12¼". c. 1880.

PLATE 67

Iridescent clear crystal vase with composite gold-enamel scrollwork and beading, applied jewels and

coralene decoration. Height 5". c. 1880.

PLATE 68

Deep cobalt-blue vase combining composite gold-enameled branches with gold-outlined flowers. Of probable Moser origin. Marked in gold on base, "312/3." Height 4⅝". c. 1880.

PLATE 69

Three-layer cased cranberry goblet with a distinctively Moser composite gold-enamel vermicular decorative pattern. Height 4¼". c. 1880.

PLATE 70

Cranberry juice glasses of three-layer cased construction. Classical warrior busts, executed in the cameo style using opaque white enamel, form an interesting contrast to the composite gold-enamel vermicular background. Height 3⅞". c. 1880.

PLATE 71

Clear crystal plate with a recessed circular pedestal foot. Intricately detailed decor consists of brightly enameled flowers and leaves, composite gold-enamel scrolls and birds enameled in high relief. Plate is 7½" square. c. 1880.

PLATE 72

Paneled four-layer cased clear-to-green vase. Decoration consists of scrolls and palmettes in composite gold-enamel with delicate enameled flowers and beading. Height 12¼". c. 1880.

PLATE 73

Delicate composite gold-enameling complements a lightweight Bohemian crystal tumbler. Height 3¾". c. 1880.

PLATE 74

Although one gets the impression of temperature-colored glass, this unusual example is constructed from three cased layers. Smoke- to dark-green shading appears to be provided by varying the thickness of the respective layers. Composite gold-enamel scrollwork and enameled flowers indicate a Moser origin. Height 4¾". c. 1880.

PLATE 75

Representing a showcase of enamel-gilt decorative techniques, this interesting wine goblet consists of a three-layer cased and cut emerald-green stem surmounted by a clear crystal bowl decorated with gold over enamel diaper- and dot-work, gold-outlined enameled flowers and composite gold-enamel branches. Height 7½". c. 1880.

PLATE 76
Copper-blue glass decanter decorated in a characteristic Moser motif. Composite gold-enameling is primarily employed to outline and highlight the enameled elements. Height 6⅜". c. 1880.

PLATE 77
Copper-blue glass vase with pale-amber handles. Enameled flowers and insects are outlined in gold. Height 6¼". c. 1880.

PLATE 78
Three-layer cased cranberry vase with a gilded clear crystal foot. Decoration consists of composite gold/silver-enamel foliate scrollwork, delicately enameled flowers and gilded rigaree. Height 8⅞". c. 1880.

PLATE 79
Resplendent in contrasting decorative motifs, this vase presents a most striking appearance. Composed of a clear crystal foot and a three-layer cased cranberry body, the large composite gold-enamel flowers complement the brightly enameled grape leaves and applied glass grapes. Whereas applied decoration was generally fused directly to a glass ground, in this example the glass beads were fused to a gilded ground. As a consequence of the reduced adhesion, a large number of beads are missing. Height 14⅝". c. 1880.

PLATE 80
Olive glass bowl with applied acorns. Comparatively rare gold and silver oak leaves are outlined with composite gold-enamel. Height 3⅜". c. 1880.

PLATE 81
Cranberry decanter in three cased layers. Gilded brass mounts, high relief flowers and composite gold-enamel Rococo scrollwork accent a well-balanced decorative form. Height 11¾". c. 1880.

PLATE 82
Clear crystal vase with a gilded ground framing iridescent red-stained windows. High relief enameled flowers, enameled leaves and composite gold-enamel scrollwork and beading complete a most attractive motif. Height 11⅞". c. 1880.

PLATE 83
Three-layer cased cranberry juice glass and demitasse

cup and saucer. High-relief enameled flowers, enameled leaves and composite gold-enamel branches on a gilded ground provide a dramatic decorative theme. Height of juice glass, 4". c. 1880.

PLATE 84
Cornucopia vase in clear crystal. Vermicular pattern in composite gold-purple enamel is highlighted by brightly enameled leaves and flowers. Height 5½". c. 1880.

PLATES 85A & 85B
Of comparative rarity, this perfume bottle, encased in the shell of an egg, would complement the most sophisticated dressing table. Decoration consists of gold paneling, composite gold-enamel leaves and foliate scrollwork and brightly enameled flowers applied to a clear crystal form which has a smoked-red stain applied to its interior. A gilded brass inner ring supports the removable perfume bottle. Height 5". c. 1880.

PLATE 86
Facet-cut tapered conical glass forms were a favorite of Moser decorators. This clear crystal vase features enameled strawberries and flowers combined with composite gold-enameling. Height is 10¼". c. 1880.

PLATE 87
Copper-blue glass box with hinged lid and brass mounts. Composite gold-enamel strawberries and butterflies are distinctively Moser. Height 5⅜". c. 1880.

PLATE 88
Lidded box of unusual design. Clear crystal base has an opaque-white enameled interior and an enameled facial exterior. Green glass hinged lid, in the form of a hat, has composite gold-enameling strongly indicating a Moser origin. Height 5". c. 1880.

PLATE 89
Unusual flower-form vase, constructed from three cased layers of uranium-doped ruby uranium-doped glass, shading from a greenish stem to a ruby bowl. Composite gold-enamel decor on a gilded ground strongly points to a Moser origin. Height 11¼". c. 1880.

PLATE 90
Amberina paneled vase enameled in Large Floral

Enameling style. Signed in script, "Moser." Height 8". c. 1890.

PLATE 91

Coralene, in the form of ground-glass chips, is employed for banding and flower petals on this finely sculptured vase. Formed from three layers of cased glass, this cranberry example incorporates the unusual feature of a woodland scene executed in opaque white enamel. Of probable Moser origin. Height 11". c. 1890.

PLATE 92

Clear crystal decanter with composite gold-enamel floral scrolls and transparent green shamrocks. Height 10". c. 1890.

PLATE 93

A cut-crystal stem surmounted by a cased cranberry bowl, exquisitely detailed enameling and a well-balanced design highlight this exceptional wine goblet. Height 7⅞". c. 1890.

PLATE 94

An exquisite example of Moser cutting and enameling techniques. This cordial has shaded gold leaves and enameled insects outlined in composite gold-enamel. Although unsigned, it bears a Moser paper label (Figure 21). Height 4½". c. 1880.

PLATE 95

Finely detailed floral work and scrollwork dominate the decor of this jeweled Rhine-wine style goblet. The ribbed base, banded in gold, is surmounted by a three-layer cased bowl, shaded clear to green. Height 8⅜". c. 1880.

PLATE 96

Composite gold-enamel Rococo scrollwork interlaced with white enamel creates a most attractive decorative motif. This small goblet has a three-layer cased clear-to-citrone bowl and a cut Bohemian crystal foot and stem. Height 4". c. 1880.

PLATE 97

Three-layer cased cranberry goblet with gilded prunts. Intricate enameled flowers and composite gold-enamel leaves and stems dominate the decorative motif. Alternate panels surrounding the bowl contain silver foliate scrolls on a gilded ground. Height 8". c. 1880. Compliments of Mr. and Mrs. William Baker.

PLATE 98

Goblet with three-layer cased cranberry bowl on a clear-crystal foot and stem. Decorated primarily with enameled flowers and composite gold-enamel floral and foliate motifs, it has been said that the stylized "H" in the foreground stands for "Hapsburg" (this attribution seems questionable in light of the fact that the "H" is found in both an open and closed form). Height 6⅛". c. 1880.

PLATE 99

Chalice with clear crystal open foot and hollow baluster stem; cranberry bowl is formed from three cased layers. Composite gold-enamel swirling branches and leaves, with finely enameled flowers, compose a typical Moser decorative form. Height 9¾". c. 1890.

PLATE 100

Three-layer cased rubina cup and saucer exhibiting intricate and finely detailed composite gold-enamel scrollwork and enameled flowers. Plate is 5½" in diameter. c. 1880.

PLATE 101

Rubina cup and saucer in three-layer cased glass. Composite gold-enamel scrollwork, floral swags and medallions decorate this intricately detailed example. Saucer is 5½" in diameter. Signed in script, "Moser." c. 1880.

PLATE 102

Cup and saucer in apple-green glass decorated with composite gold- and silver-enamel flowers; cup has blown-out mellon ribbing. Saucer is 5½" in diameter. Signed in script, "Moser." c. 1880.

PLATE 103

Rigaree-footed rubina vase in three-layer cased glass. Unusual applied glass hobnails complement a free-flowing floral pattern executed in white and orange enamels. Height 6". Signed in enameled block letters, "MOSER KARLSBAD AUSTRIA." c. 1900.

PLATE 104

Intricately detailed wine goblet with a three-layer cased pale-ruby bowl and clear crystal foot and stem. Enameled motif features composite gold-enamel leaves and branches and composite silver-enamel flowers. Height 7¼". c. 1890.

PLATE 105
Gold paneling and composite gold-enamel foliate scrollwork on a dark-green glass ground provides an interesting study in contrast. This example probably dates from the 1880's but could easily have been produced during the first quarter of the 20th century. Height 6⅝".

PLATE 106
Three amber-stained clear crackel-glass vases decorated with enameled aquatic and floral motifs. Height of vase on left is 4⅞". c. 1890.

PLATE 107
Paneled blue glass decanter set of typical Bohemian form. Large Floral Enameling style reflects a definite Art Nouveau influence. Decanter height is 8¾"; tray is 9" in diameter. Signed in script, "Moser." c. 1890.

PLATE 108
Finely executed finger bowl and underplate in copper-blue glass. Underplate is 6" across flats. c. 1890.

PLATE 109
Gourd-shaped clear-to-amethyst vase in three cased layers. Monochrome enameled figure of a warrior concealed by sweeping foliage of Art Nouveau form. Height 7¾". Acid-etched signature, "Glasfabrik Karlsbad." c. 1895.

PLATE 110
Clear-crystal Art Nouveau sherbert and underplate decorated with transparent enamels outlined in gold. Saucer is 4½" in diameter. Signed in script, "Moser." c. 1900.

PLATE 111
Acid-finished vase in opaque-white glass with gilded brass mounts. Composite gold-enamel floral motif stands out in bold relief. Attributed to Moser. Height 8½". c. 1900.

PLATE 112
Deeply engraved Art Nouveau perfume bottle and vase of amethyst shading (five cased layers). As is characteristic of most Moser examples, the engraved design is also present on the clear crystal stopper. Height of vase is 3½". Vase is signed in script, "Moser Karlsbad." c. 1900.

PLATE 113
Cobalt-blue deeply engraved Art Nouveau lidded box

of five-layer cased construction. Box is 4⅛" square by 3¼" high. c. 1900.

PLATE 114
Unusual clear to emerald-green deeply engraved Art Nouveau vase of five cased layers. Eight facet-cut sides are decorated with intaglio-cut wild roses complemented by high-relief enameled vines, leaves and insects; insect bodies are formed from glass beading. Height 14". c. 1900. Compliments of Alice Kwartler.

PLATE 115
Comparatively rare clear-to-ruby deeply engraved Art Nouveau decanter constructed from three cased layers. Height 13½". c. 1900.

PLATE 116
Bohemian crystal champagne with deeply engraved Art Nouveau wild roses. Foot and rim are decorated with an intaglio-cut and gilded band of rose buds and stems. Height 7". c. 1900.

PLATE 117
Deeply engraved Art Nouveau vase with cameo-cut cased red-over-green floral inset. Two-cased-layer brown-clear-brown shading is of a comparatively rare color. Height 4½". Engraved signature, "Moser Karlsbad." c. 1900.

PLATE 118
Deeply engraved Art Nouveau goblet with cameo-cut amber glass floral inset. Unusual construction features a three-layer cased pale-ruby foot, a clear crystal stem and a two-layer cased shaded pale-ruby bowl. Height 8⅝". c. 1900.

PLATE 119
Deeply engraved Art Nouveau vase with a cameo-cut purple glass iris inset. Unusual four-cased layer amethyst-clear-amethyst shading serves to accent the floral focal point. Height 6⅞". Engraved signature, "Moser Karlsbad." c. 1900. Compliments of David's Antiques.

PLATE 120
Clear crystal Karlsbader Secession decanter with green and red glass insets, intaglio-cut birds and insects, translucent enameling and high-relief enameled and gilded branches. Height 16¾". c. 1900.

PLATE 121
Contrasting Art Nouveau forms. c. 1900. Left to

right, clear-to-amethyst deeply engraved beaker; signed in script, "Moser"; height 4½". Amethyst-to-clear engraved vase attributed to Graf Harrach.

PLATE 122

Green-to-clear Art Nouveau vase with engraving highlighted in gold. Rim and base borders are enamel covered with gold. Signed in gold, "Harrach." Height 4½". c. 1900.

PLATE 123

Of comparative rarity, this Bohemian crystal vase is engraved in a typical Moser Art Nouveau motif. Height 9¾". c. 1900.

PLATE 124

Paneled clear-to-amethyst three-layer cased cologne bottle and decanter with matched composite gold-enamel decorative themes. Height of decanter is 9¼". Cologne bottle has acid-etched signature, "Glasfabric Karlsbad." c. 1895.

PLATE 125

A pair of tapered eight-sided facet-cut vases in clear-to-amethyst and clear to smoke-white shading. Exhibiting a similar composite gold-enamel decorative motif, the glass blanks for these vases were probably produced at Meierhöfen. Height 7⅜". c. 1895.

PLATE 126

Emerald-green to clear shading, combined with composite gold-enamel foliate scrolls, produce a striking visual effect. Saucer and bowl are of three-layer cased construction, while the foot and handle of the cup are clear crystal. c. 1900.

PLATE 127

Clear to emerald-green three-layer cased decanter. Composite gold-enamel palmettes and scrolls emphasize the mellon-ribbed base and are echoed on the neck and stopper. Height 10". Acid-etched signature "Glasfabrik Karlsbad made in Austria." c. 1910.

PLATE 128

Pale-brown glass paneled vase with two applied enameled glass fish on a background of enameled aquatic plants. Quality of the glass blank would indicate a Meierhöfen origin. Height 5¼". c. 1910.

PLATE 129

Rubina-verde two-layer cased glass. c. 1910. Left to right, vertical facet-cut pitcher with pink-amber handle; composite gold-enamel Rococo foliate scrolls and floral bouquets on raised oval panels; height 7⅝". Paneled vase with gilded rigaree handles; composite gold-enamel fern-like leaves and flowers; signed in script, "Moser"; height 11". Facet-cut baluster bud vase with panels outlined in gold; height 6¾". Glass of this type was probably manufactured at Meier-höfen.

PLATE 130

Rainbow glass vase in multiple colors of blue, yellow and red. Gilded rim has white enamel foliate scrolls accented in black. Height 7". c. 1910.

PLATE 131

An impressive dark-amber cut to light-amber vase. Acid cut-back jungle scene displays gilded highlights on an ungilded ground; typical of earlier Moser work of this type. Height 13¾". Signed in gilded cameo, "Moser Karlsbad; RW; MK." Courtesy of Oscar Ghebelian.

PLATE 132

Amethyst cameo vase featuring lions in a jungle setting. Acid-cut highlights are gilded on an ungilded background. Height 6". c. 1910.

PLATE 133

Hot Punch set in clear crystal featuring vertical mitre cuts and a facet-cut pedestal. Apex of mitre-cut is zipper-cut and gilded; trough of mitre-cut has finely gilded lining. Punch bowl lid is decorated with composite gold-enamel foliate scrolls in a star pattern. Height of bowl, including cover, is 13½". Each piece is signed, "Glasfabrik Karlsbad made in Austria." c. 1910.

PLATE 134

Demitasse cup and saucer in clear crystal. Decorative motif of transparent enameled flowers probably dates from the early 1900's. Signed in script, "Moser."

PLATE 135

Gray-green crystal tray with chevron-decorated rim. Bold floral decoration is executed in shaded gold outlined with composite gold-enamel. Diameter is 8⅞". Large acid-etched signature, "Moser Karlsbad." c. 1910.

PLATE 136

This beautiful pair of paneled pink-amethyst vases are enameled in a floral motif reminiscent of that

produced by Thomas Webb & Sons. Height 6".
c. 1910.

PLATE 137
Deep-amethyst covered box on four ball feet. Acid-cut-back decorative border and frieze of Amazon warriors are completely gilded. Box is 4⅞" in diameter. Signed in script, "Moser Karlsbad." c. 1920.

PLATE 138
Gold Topaz decanter set with Modern-style facet cutting. Although of matched design, the decanter has an acid-cut-back frieze of Amazon warriors while the cordials feature satyrs and nymphs. Height of decanter is 12". c. 1920.

PLATE 139
Facet and diamond cutting, combined with gilded floral engraving, produce an appealing overall effect. The pale-pink amber glass of which this example is constructed was probably produced at Meierhöfen. Height 8¼". c. 1920.

PLATE 140
Pansy vases decorated in the Large Floral Enameling style with flecked gold rims. Each vase is of paneled three-layer cased construction. Vase on left is 14⅜" high and is signed in script, "Moser." c. 1920.

PLATE 141
Ribbed cranberry decanter in three-layer cased glass with pinched sides and applied prunts. Mold-blown stopper and foot are clear crystal. Prunts are covered with an orange-amber translucent enamel. Enameled flowers are outlined in gold enamel typical of this decorative style. Height 10". c. 1920.

PLATE 142
Paneled clear-to-amethyst vase of three cased layers. Large Floral Enameling decorative style is embellished by the addition of gilded bees and a flecked gold rim. Height 11½". Signed in script, "Moser"; base bears original Moser-Czechoslovakia paper label. c. 1920.

PLATE 143
Three examples of fanciful enameling on glassware probably destined for the Spanish market. c. 1920. Left to right, clear crystal vase signed in gold, "ROYO." Green glass decanter with lamp-work swan finial on cork stopper; signed in gold, "Cire." Vase

with gold-amber bowl and clear crystal foot; signed in gold, "ROYO"; height 6".

PLATE 144
Amethyst paneled vase with applied and enameled blue glass fish. Enameled leaves and flowers are outlined in gold. Note the stylistic change from the earlier more naturalistic forms. Height 5¼". c. 1910.

PLATE 145
Bohemian crystal vase decorated with black enamel figural of girl and goats. Central motif is surrounded by a gilded acid-cut-back cartouche with enameled floral highlights. Height 8". Signed in enamel, "Moser Karlsbad." c. 1920.

PLATE 146
Bohemian crystal pedistal vase with facet, zipper and fan cutting. Foot and bowl are accented with composite gold-enamel flowers, palmettes and scrolls. Height 14⅛". c. 1920.

PLATE 147
Compared to 19th-century examples, this Bohemian crystal vase has a rather subtle appearance. Upon close examination, however, the finely executed composite gold-enamel foliate scrollwork and starburst cut panels reveal a well-balanced and appealing decorative form typical of 20th-century Moser. Height 11⅞". c. 1920.

PLATE 148
Starburst cutting on a three-layer cased cranberry bowl, composite gold-enamel foliate scrollwork and a twisted solid stem of Bohemian crystal is characteristically 20th-century Moser. Height 8½". c. 1920.

PLATE 149
Finger bowl and underplate in clear Bohemian crystal. Although the enamel and composite gold-enamel decorative pattern is based on 19th-century design, this example probably dates from the 1920's.

PLATE 150
Lead crystal sherbet with radial mitre-cutting on the base, a facet-cut knop and a zipper-cut stem. A gilded acid-cut-back floral pattern decorates the bowl. Height 5⅛". c. 1920.

PLATE 151
A most elegant decanter set in the "Royal" pattern (No. 9000) emblazoned with the monogram of a

prominent New England family. Height of decanter is 10¾". c. 1920.

PLATE 152
Light-olive glass vase with applied circular handles. Gracefully flowing floral forms are enameled and outlined in gold. Height 9⅞". Script signature "Moser" on body; base has original Moser-Czechoslovakia paper label. c. 1920.

PLATE 153
Opaque-white over pale-amethyst overlay vase. Cut-through areas are outlined in gold; enameled flowers are outlined in black. Height 9¼". Acid-etched signature, "Moser Karlsbad." c. 1920. Compliments of Mr. and Mrs. David Fry.

PLATE 154
Molded vases probably based on a design executed by Josef Hoffman. Left to right: malachite glass signed "Moser Karlsbad"; unsigned lead crystal. Height 5". c. 1920.

PLATE 155
Chalice having a clear crystal trumpet foot and hollow stem; shaded clear-to-citrone machine-threaded bowl is composed of three cased layers. Overall decorative balance and composite gold-enamel foliate scrollwork points to a c. 1920 Moser origin. Height 9³⁄₁₆".

PLATE 156
Clear crystal cup and saucer and goblet with heavy Baroque scrollwork formed in high relief; separately fired gold over enamel. These examples show the use of gold backing on the inside glass surface to block the visibility of the enamel undercoat. Cup and saucer have stained ruby panels with flowers and monogram; goblet has extremely fine enameled flowers. Saucer is 5¼" in diameter; goblet is 6" high. Cup and saucer both have acid-etched signature, "Moser Karlsbad." c. 1925.

PLATE 157
Clear crystal cup and saucer decorated in a gilded stylized fish scale motif. c. 1920.

PLATE 158
Copper-blue glass vase decorated with large brightly enameled roses and applied gilded bees. Height 11¾". Signed in script, "Moser." c. 1920.

PLATE 159
Dinnerware featuring brightly enameled Acanthus scrollwork. Wine and dessert plate to left were part of a set originally made by Moser for Tiffany & Co., New York. Small plate is 6⅜" in diameter. c. 1925.

PLATE 160
Alexandrit facet-cut compote, free-formed vase and display mark. Compote is 4" high. c. 1925. Compliments of Mr. and Mrs. Harry Foreman.

PLATE 161
Alexandrit decanter set in the "Thomas" pattern (No. 14000). Decanter height is 7⅜". Acid-etched signature, "Alexandrit-Moser Karlsbad." c. 1925.

PLATE 162
Beryll Modern-cut cologne bottle (Cat. No. W9773). Acid-etched signature, "Moser." Height 5". c. 1925.

PLATE 163
Pair of Royalit cordials cut in the Modern style. Height 4⅛". Acid-etched signature, "Moser." c. 1925.

PLATE 164
Left to right, free-formed Heliolit ashtray; 6" in length. Free-formed Beryll vase; height 5½". c. 1925. Compliments of Mr. and Mrs. Harry Foreman.

PLATE 165
Alexandrit cologne bottle with hollow stopper. Height 5⅜". Acid-etched signature, "Moser," as well as Meyr's Neffe affixed paper label. c. 1925.

PLATE 166
Polished Alexandrit plaque engraved with wild roses. Height 6⅛". Signed in script, "Moser Karlsbad orig. Allexandrit"; artist signed, "K. Hable." c. 1925.

PLATE 167
Designed by Stefan Rath after an original model in the Prague Museum, this clear crystal goblet with baluster stem and engraved woodland scene is part of Lobmeyr table set No. 253 (still in production). Height 7¾". Signed with script "Moser" and engraved Lobmeyr signature at base of scene. c. 1925.

PLATE 168
Bohemian crystal chalice with green and ruby glass marquetry and engraved leaves. Base of chalice bears a Meyr's Neffe paper label. Height 10¼". c. 1925.

PLATE 169
Spiral mitre and flute cutting accent the beauty of this Eldor vase. Height 4¾". c. 1925. Compliments of Mr. and Mrs. Harry Foreman.

PLATE 170
Free-formed and cut examples of Moser's ruby glass. Free-formed ashtray was a gift given by Leo Moser to his close friends at his 50th birthday party and is dated 1929. Vase is 7½" high. Compliments of Mr. and Mrs. Harry Foreman.

PLATE 171
Gold Topaz Art Deco bureau set; a gift from Leo Moser to his daughter, Lea. Large bottle is 7" high. Compliments of Mr. and Mrs. Harry Foreman.

PLATE 172
Facet-cut Art Deco dresser set consisting of an atomizer, cologne bottle and a lidded box. Acid-etched "Moser Karlovy Vary, made in Czec-oslovakia" signature. Height of cologne is 5". c. 1920.

PLATE 173
Art Deco smoke-amber decanter. Height 19½". Acid-etched signature, "Moser, made in Czechoslovakia." c. 1925.

PLATE 174
Smoke-olive-colored beaker typifying the Modern style of cutting employed by Moser. Height 5¼". c. 1925.

PLATE 175
An important amethyst Art Deco vase with a Renaissance-style figural grouping executed in oroide (an alloy containing copper, tin, etc., used to imitate gold) and applied with a gravure photochemical printing process. Height 11⅜". Personally signed by Leo Moser, "Orogravur, Moser Karlsbad, Leo"; dated 1924. Compliments of Mr. and Mrs. Harry Foreman.

PLATE 176
Modern-style cut vase in "Radon" glass with acid-cut-back frieze of Amazon warriors. Signed in script, "Made in Czechoslovakia, Moser Karlsbad." Height 7⅜". c. 1925.

PLATE 177
Moser glass samples from the 1895-1933 period. Left to right: Ruby, dated 4/12/29; Alexandrit; W89, dated 8/1/29; Amethyst; D. W. Blau; Lavendblau, dated 12/2/30; Giftgrün; Beryll; and Lichtbryl, dated 11/10/30. Compliments of Mr. and Mrs. Harry Foreman.

PLATE 178
More Moser glass samples from the 1895-1933 period. Left to right: Heliolit, W119; Heliolit; Gold Topaz; Praseomit; Rossgrün; Oliv; L. W. Altgrün, dated 1/6/30; and Ozeangrün. Compliments of Mr. and Mrs. Harry Foreman.

PLATE 179
Art Deco emerald-green bowl with acid-cut-back cameo aquatic motif. Height 7". Acid-etched signature, "Moser TCECHO-SLOVAQUIE." c. 1920. Compliments of Mr. and Mrs. George Redtman.

PLATE 180
Words fail to adequately describe the simplistic beauty of this Modern-cut goblet; ruby bowl is composed of three case layers. Acid-etched signature, "Moser." Height 7¾". c. 1925.

PLATE 181
Facet-cut bowl in a deep-blue glass developed by Moser exclusively for the Wiener Werkstätte. Initial design was probably by Josef Hoffman. Acid-etched Wiener Werkstätte/Moser signature (Figure 20). c. 1925. Compliments of the Prague Museum of Decorative Arts (inventory no. 85.542).

PLATE 182
Cameo tableware with raised and gilded foliate scrolls, rocaille and grape clusters on an acid-cut-back stippled ground. Of comparative rarity, the pedestal foot of the sherbet, as well as the stem and foot of the goblet, are lead crystal. Plate signed in script, "Moser." Height of goblet is 4¾". c. 1930.

PLATE 183
Stylized wedding cup in opaque black glass designed by Fritzi Löw-Lazar of the Wiener Werkstätte. Height 6". Acid-etched signature, "Moser, made in Czecho-slovakia." c. 1930.

PLATE 184
Iridescent patterned clear crystal pitcher. Height 7¼". Light acid-etched signature on base executed in capital letters, "CRISTALLERI KARLOVY VARY MOSER," artist signed "RICHE." c. 1925.

PLATE 185
Amethyst footed bowl with Art Deco fine-line decorative pattern acid-cut and gilded. Height 3¾". c. 1925.

PLATE 186
Facet-cut vase in smoke-gray crystal. Height 6". c. 1925.

PLATE 187
From the high-relief floral decoration, surrounded by a cartouche of translucent enamel and beading, to the composite gold-enamel scrollwork and applied jewels, this clear crystal vase represents an exceptionally fine example of enameled artistic glass. Height 8½". c. 1925.

PLATE 188
Distinctively decorated in the Moser style with composite gold-enamel foliate scrolls, high-relief flowers and applied jewels, this acid-etched clear crystal tumbler bears a gold Lobmeyr signature. Evidence suggests that this item was manufactured for Lobmeyr by the Moser glassworks. Height 3 $\frac{7}{16}$". c. 1925.

PLATE 189
Clear crystal chalice of magnificent proportions accented with red and blue jewels. This example is typical of the fine enameled glass produced by Moser after WW I. Height 12¼".

PLATE 190
Clear crystal syrup pitcher with enameled flowers, composite gold-enamel ferns and a diamond-cut waistband accented with gold lines. Height 3⅞". c. 1925.

PLATE 191
Clear crystal beer glass decorated with applied jewels, transparent enameled leaves, gold and silver over enamel Rococo scrollwork and composite gold-enamel drops. Molded rock-like base is interlaced with gold lines. Height 5¾". c. 1925.

PLATE 192
Pale-green goblet with a beaded hollow stem; knop is decorated with gilded prunts and red faceted jewels on a fine coralene ground. Finely detailed composite gold-enamel grape leaves and vines combined with composite silver-enamel grapes complete a most striking design. Height 8". c. 1925.

PLATE 193
Facet-cut vase in Oliv crystal. Height 6½". Acid-etched signature, "Moser Karlsbad." c. 1930.

PLATE 194
Various formulas for lead crystal appear in the Moser factory melt journal. This elegant example is decorated with a gilded acid-cut-back Rococo and floral pattern essentially identical to one employed by the Honesdale Decorating Co. during the 1902-08 time period. Hinged silver lid is marked with the German "800; Crown & Crescent." Height 12". c. 1930.

PLATE 195
Elements of a clear crystal cocktail set acquired from the Czech legation in New York City. Each piece has a facet-cut paperweight base and is highlighted by an acid-cut-back and gilded cockfight. Height of shaker is 10". Acid-etched signature, "Moser." c. 1930. Compliments of Mr. and Mrs. Chan Robinson.

PLATE 196
Ruby plate decorated in the typical "Venetian" style. 7¼" in diameter. Signed in script, "Moser." c. 1930.

PLATE 197
Footed charger in ruby glass decorated in the "Venetian" style. Enameled signature on the base rim, "MURANO." Diameter, 14½". c. 1930.

PLATE 198
Clear to cobalt-blue paneled decanter formed from five cased layers. Baroque Zwischengold-type decoration is applied to, what appears to be, a typical Bohemian glass form. Height 11⅜". Attributed to Pauly & Cia., Venice. c. 1920.

PLATE 199
Representing a nearly exact copy of an enameled pattern found on 16th-17th-century Spanish glass, examples of the type shown here and in Plate 200 are occasionally found bearing a script Moser signature. The sherbet and underplate are executed in Venetian-type clear crystal. c. 1925.

PLATE 200
See Plate 199. This footed goblet is of a heavier facet-cut form. It is 5⅞" high. c. 1925.

PLATE 201
Alexandrit vase exhibiting one of the many facet-cutting styles employed by Moser to enhance the jewel-like properties of their rare-earth-doped glasses. Acid-etched "Moser Karlsbad" signature. Height 4". c. 1930.

PLATE 202
Alexandrit shallow vase with concave facet cutting in the Modern art glass style of the 1930's. Height 4½". c. 1930.

PLATE 203
Bohemian crystal pedestal vase cut in the Modern style. Height 10⅛″. c. 1930. Compliments of Mr. and Mrs. Ludwig Moser.

PLATE 204
Unbreakable clear glass tumbler signed "Dural." Height 3½″. c. 1930. Compliments of Mr. and Mrs. Harry Foreman.

PLATE 205
Molded vase of Bohemian crystal. Height 8⅓″. c. 1930. Compliments of Mr. and Mrs. Harry Foreman.

PLATE 206
Composite Alexandrit-Bohemian crystal molded vase in the "Chipped Ice" pattern. Height 6⅝″. c. 1930. Compliments of Mr. and Mrs. Harry Foreman.

X. MOSER IN PERSPECTIVE

Within a comparatively short period of 76 years, the firm of Ludwig Moser and Sons ascended from the drab surroundings of a spa engraving studio to become a world celebrated supplier of artistic glass. Through an international network of fine shops, Moser sold luxury glassware to socially prominent and wealthy patrons and included among its customers crowned heads in Europe and the Middle East. Even though Ludwig Moser was recognized by his contemporaries as a painter and engraver of significant stature, his greater achievement was as a glassmaker. The Moser firm's unparalleled success was the direct result of Ludwig's personal dedication to the production of glassware of uncompromising quality.

During the period between 1857 and 1895, glass marketed by Moser consisted of highly distinctive decorative motifs applied to glass blanks purchased from major Bohemian glasshouses. Success abroad was ensured by an extensive network of glass merchandising centers, while, at home, the appointment of Ludwig Moser as "Supplier of Glass" to the Austrian Imperial Court of Franz Joseph solidified his position as a major Bohemian manufacturer of artistic glass.

1895 witnessed the completion of Moser's glassworks at Meierhöfen and with it a major shift in emphasis away from the production of intricately enameled glassware. Technical perfection of the glass melt and forming process, development of complementary cutting and engraving techniques and the introduction of new colored glass formulations became an all-consuming passion. Such dedication to excellence was rewarded by a high level of visibility at international competitions and a seemingly endless procession of socially prominent patrons.

In 1922, the Moser firm, under the artistic directorship of Leo Moser, purchased Meyr's Neffe's Adolf works in southern Bohemia. Although Moser produced decorative glassware designed by the noted Art Deco artist Joseph Hoffman prior to World War I, the acquisition of Meyr's Neffe opened the door to the full design capability of the Wiener Werkstätte association of artists. Beginning with the fourth quarter of the 19th century, Meyr's Neffe had been the major supplier of enameled glass to the celebrated firm J.&L. Lobmeyr. After the merger, Moser lost little time in capitalizing on this expertise. As the result of the combined design and artistic resources of the two firms, enameled glassware marketed by Moser regained, and in some aspects surpassed, its former splendor.

At Meierhofen, Leo Moser continued the development of richly colored glasses and, in 1922, was the first to introduce commercial production of rare-earth doped glasses. Advanced prismatic cutting styles designed to enhance the jewel-like properties of these new glasses won international acclaim. These achievements, in combination with the fact that glass cutters and engravers retained by the Moser firm were recognized as among the finest available in Central Europe, attracted the attention of local and internationally prominent glass artists and designers. During the 1920's, Moser became a forum of contemporary design. Uniquely designed glassware, representing a significant departure from traditional Moser product lines, was commissioned in quantity and, in many instances, it too found its way into international competitions. Artistic glass produced by the Moser firm during the two decades following World War I reached a pinnacle of design and technical execution which remains unsurpassed up to the present day.

A GATHERING OF COLLECTORS

Collectors are a curious lot. Whether the object sought be a Philadelphia Chippendale secretary or a lowly matchbox cover, the challenge is approached with an equal level of enthusiasm. Driven by an insatiable urge to possess the finest or most extensive collection possible, to say nothing of the dream of finding a "sleeper" hidden in some obscure byway, collectors gradually develop an advanced knowledge of their subject which many times exceeds that possessed by recognized scholars. In the absence of reliable written documentation, information gained through this type of "hands on" experience can prove quite valuable. In a like manner, antique dealers, driven by the desire to be well informed about the articles they sell, often develop an extensive storehouse of knowledge within their areas of specialization.

The authors have a mutual acquaintance who, for years after graduation from college, exhibited little or no interest in antiques or collecting. During this time, his wife, belligerently besieged by demands to stay home and stop wasting money, frequented auction houses and antique shops in the hope that eventually her husband would see the error in his ways. Fueled at first by the recognition that antiques not only provide visual enjoyment but also retain their monitary value, a spark of interest belatedly began to grow. One day, while rummaging through a local outdoor antique market, our friend came across a retired collector who was selling his most treasured possessions. Two beautifully enameled pieces of glass quickly attracted his attention. "Who produced this glassware?" our friend inquired. "Moser!" came the immediate reply. Love at first sight almost seems inadequate to describe the dramatic change engendered by those two pieces of glass. For, within a short period of time, the collecting of Moser glass became an all-consuming passion. Rather than purchase expensive examples from the recognized mainstream of Moser production, our friend wisely concentrated on collecting lesser known samples. Fourteen years later, his extensive collection of Moser glass and the subsequent knowledge gained through its acquisition have provided an invaluable backdrop to the writing of this book.

In presenting the material contained within these pages we have tried to be as factual as possible. In some cases, however, conclusions drawn reflect the blending of documented evidence with deductive reasoning. Historical accounts were largely assembled from published information and, as such, are dependent for their accuracy on the original material. Records brought to the United States by Leo Moser can be considered "firsthand" information. But, here also, notes concerning the history of the Moser firm prior to 1916 were not contemporary with their occurrence and are consequently subject to lapses in memory. Finally, a large portion of the glass samples presented in this book are of a type readily available to the American collector. Given Moser's penchant for catering to specialized geographical markets, these articles may well be considered rare in other parts of the world.

We present this book as a necessary step in assembling a comprehensive body of information concerning the history and artistic output of the Moser firm; however, many gray areas still exist, and it is to these subjects that we must address our future investigative efforts. Past geopolitical conditions, in combination with the diversity exhibited by Moser products, severly restrict the gathering of new information. Factory catalogs or sales brochures issued by branch offices represent a valuable source of information; unfortunately, the existence of such items or their whereabouts remains an open question. It appears probable that the bulk of Moser factory records, with the exception of those brought to this country by Leo Moser, were destroyed during World War II, and it is unlikely that any new documentation of significant size will be uncovered. Rather, it will be necessary to identify and authenticate small pockets of information and integrate them into the existing historical framework. Collectors, whether in reference to physical or intellectual pursuits, represent the front line of attack in surmounting these roadblocks. It is to these individuals that we appeal by requesting that any new information, no matter how small or seemingly insignificant, be brought to the authors' attention.

One final thought: Let glass historians sift through dusty archives and argue over the authenticity of this and that. At best, such activities represent but a complementary diversion from the real significance of artistic glass. At once a unique harmonization of function and aesthetic appeal, fine glass is a lofty expression of artistic ideals which entreats those who possess it to sit back, relax and enjoy.

BIBLIOGRAPHY

Adressbuch Europas Glasindustrie. Herausgegeben von der Redaktion der Zeilschrift: "Die Glashütte." Dresden, 1925.

Arwas, Victor. *Glass — Art Nouveau to Art Deco.* New York: Rizzoli Int. Pub. Inc., 1980.

Blau, Josef. *Die Glasmacher in Böhmer-und Bayer-wald.* Regensburg: im Verlag Michael Lassleben Kallmunz, 1956.

Bloch-Dermant, Janine. *The Art of French Glass, 1860-1914.* New York: The Vendome Press, 1974.

Bröhan, Sammlung Karl H. "Kunsthandwerk — Glas Holz Keramik." Berlin, 1976.

Buckley, W. *European Glass.* New York: Hought Mifflin Co., 1926.

Campana, D.M. "Enamel Decorations for Porcelain and Glass," *Campana's Popular Art Library,* 2nd ed., 1947.

Českísklo, XIX stoleti, Moravska Galerie V. Brnê, Červen-Žař, 1979.

Charon, Mural K. *Ludwig (Ludvik) Moser — King of Glass.* Hillsdale, Mich.: Charon/Ferguson-Division of Ferguson Communications, Pub., 1984.

The Corning Museum of Glass. *Czechoslovakian Glass.* New York: Dover Publications, 1981.

The Crystalex Branch Corporation. *Bohemian Glass.* Nový Bor, 1985.

Cox, Claude V. *Ludwig Moser — Royal Glass Artisan.* Decatur, Ill.: Coxes Collectables, 1978.

Davis, Frank. *Antique Glass and Glass Collecting.* London: Hamlyn Pub. Group, Ltd., 1973.

Drahotova, Olga. *European Art Glass.* New York: Excalibur Books, 1983.

Fahdt, Julius. *Die Glasindustrie Oesterreich-Ungarns.* Dresden: Selbstverlag, 1901.

Feller, John Quentin. "Katharine Louise Dorflinger: Christian Dorflinger's Daughter and Heir," *The National Early American Glass Club Bulletin,* No. 148 (Winter 1985/86).

Garner, Philippe, ed. *The Encyclopedia of Decorative Arts.* New York: Van Nostrand Reinhold Co., 1979.

Gilard, P. et. al. "The Flourescence of Glass," *The Glass Industry,* March 1938 (New York).

"Glas, Historismus und die Historismen um 1900," Staatliche Musee zu Berlin, Kunstgewerbemuseum Schlob Köpenick, Nov. 1977.

Gros-Galliner, Gabriella. *Glass — A Guide for Collectors.* New York: Stein and Day Publishers, 1970.

Grover, Lee and Ray. *Art Glass Nouveau.* Rutland, Vt.: Charles E. Tuttle Co., 1967.

Grover, Lee and Ray. *European Art Glass.* Rutland, Vt.: Charles E. Tuttle Co., 1970.

Gruber, Sammlung H.R. "Jugend stilglas," Mittelrheinisches Landesnaseum, Mainz, 1976.

Gysling-Billeter, Erika. *Objekte des Jugendstils.* Bern: Benteli Verlag, 1975.

Hájek, Jindřich. "Karlovy Vary — The Cradle of the 'Glass of Kings,'" *Czech. Glass Review,* Vol. 2 (1964), p. 42.

Heacock, Bill. *Glass (Collecting),* Vol. I. Antique Publications, 1985.

Hilschenz, Helga. "Das Glas des Jugendstils," Katalog der Sammlung Heutrich im Kunstmuseum Düsseldorf, Prestel-Verlag, München, 1973.

Historismus — Kunsthandwerk und Industrie im Zeitalter der Weltausstellungen," Staatliche Museen, Preussischer Kulturbesitz.

"Katalog der Kunstgewerbemuseums," Berlin Bd. VII, Berlin, 1973.

Kreidl, Norbert J. "Rare Earths," Journal of the American Ceramic Society, Vol. 25 (1942), pp. 141-143.

Kutac̄, Vincene. "120 Years of Existence of the Moser Glassworks at Karlovy Vary," *Czech. Glass Review,* Vol. 32 (1977), pp. 2-6.

Langhamer, Antonín. "Engraved Glass from the Karlovarské Sklo Glassworks," *Czech. Glass Review,* Vol. 32 (1977), pp. 7-11.

"Leerdam Unica," 50 Jahre Modernes Niederländisches Glas, Kunstmuseum Düsseldorf, 1977; Museum Boymans-van Beuningen Rotterdam, 1977.

Mackay, James. *Dictionary of Turn of the Century Antiques.* London: Wardlock Limited, 1974.

Manley, Cyril. *Decorative Victorian Glass.* New York: Van Nostrand Reinhold, 1981.

Matura, Adolf. "Moser Karlovy Vary Glass," *Czech. Glass Review,* June 1964, pp. 163-169.

McClinton, Katherine Morrison. *Art Deco—A Guide for Collectors.* New York: Clarkson N. Potter, Inc., 1972.

Middlemas, Keith. *Antique Glass in Color.* New York: Doubleday and Co., 1971.

Moser, Leo. "Commercial Art Glass," *The Glass Industry,* March 1942 (New York).

Mundt, Barbara. *Historismus.* Berlin, 1974.

Mundt, Barbara. *Historismus.* München: Keysersche Verlagsbuchhandlung, 1981.

Neuwirth, Waltraud. *Orientalisierende Gläser, J.&.L. Lobmeyr, Band 1.* Wien: Selbstverlag Dr. Waltraud Neuwirth, 1981.

Neuwirth, Waltraud. *Wiener Werkstätte.* Wien: Selbstverlag Dr. Waltraud Neuwirth, 1984.

Newman, Harold. *An Illustrated Dictionary of Glass.* London: Thames and Hudson Ltd., 1977.

Pazaurek, Gustav E. *Modern Gläser.* Leipzig: Hermann Seemann Nachfoldge, 1910.

Pazaurek, Gustav E. *Glaser der Empire—und Biedermeierzeit.* Klinkhardt und Biermann.

Pazaurek, Gustav E., and Walter Spiegl. *Glas des 20. Jahrhunderts, Jugendstil-Art Déco.* München: Klinkhardt & Biermann, 1983.

Pešatová, Zuzana. *Bohemian Engraved Glass.* Prague: Knihtisk, 1968.

Phillips, Phoebe. *The Encyclopedia of Glass.* New York: Crown Publishers, Inc., 1981.

Polak, Ada. *Glass—Its Tradition and its Makers.* New York: G.P. Putnam's Sons, 1975.

Revi, Albert Christian. *Nineteenth Century Glass.* New York: Galahad Books, 1959/1967.

Robertson, R.A. *Chat on Old Glass.* New York: Dover Publications, Inc., 1969.

Savage, George. *Glass and Glassware.* London: Octopus Books Ltd., 1973.

Schmidt, Robert. *Lobmeyer, 1823-1923.* Wien: Anton Schroll & Co.

Schuman, John A. III. *Art Glass Sampler.* Des Moines, Iowa: Wallace-Homestead, 1978.

Schweiger, Werner J. *Wiener Werkstätte-Design in Vienna, 1902-1932.* New York: Abbeville Press, 1984.

The Smithsonian Illustrated Library of Antiques. "Glass," prepared by the Cooper-Hewitt Museum, 1979.

Spiegl, Walter. *Glas des Historismus.* Braunschweig: Klinkhardt & Biermann, 1980.

"The 125th Anniversary of the Moser Glassworks at Karlovy Vary," *Czech. Glass Review,* Vol. 36 (1981), pp. 2-28.

Villain, Jean. "The History of the Bohemian Glass Blowers," Weltbuehne, Ost Berlin, March 1960.

Vose, Ruth Hurst. *Glass.* London: The Connoisseur, 1975.

Vratislav, Sotolam. "Nekonvenĉní Moser," *Domov,* No. 6 (1966), pp. 16-19.

Weiss, Gustav. *The Book of Glass.* Praeger Publishing Co., 1971.

Weyl, Woldemart. *Colored Glass.* Sheffield, England: Society of Glass Technology.

Zimmerman. "Hollandisches Glas, Glaser von Chris Lebeau," *Die Schaulade,* 1928.